NEW MISSION FOR A NEW PEOPLE

Voices From The Caribbean

DAVID I. MITCHELL

Acknowlegments

"Society and Its Tensions" (p. 95) and "Education and Its Imbalances" (p. 101) by Irene Hawkins, are excerpts from her book, *The Changing Face of the Caribbean*, published by the Cedar Press, P.O. Box 616, Bridgetown, Barbados, W.I., and used by permission.

Library of Congress Cataloging in Publication Data
Main entry under title:
New mission for a new people.

    Includes bibliographical references.
    1. Caribbean area—addresses, essays, lectures.
I. Mitchell, David I.
F2161.N47   972.9   77-2331
ISBN 0-377-00062-0

Copyright © 1977 by Friendship Press, Inc.
Printed in the United States of America

contents

Foreword	5
Introduction: A Flight into Eden?	7
Part One — The Colonial Legacy	11
The British Empire	15
David Mitchell	
Guyana	20
P.I. Gomes	
Poor Little Belize	25
Claude Cadogan	
The French Presence and the Church in Martinique and Guadeloupe	30
Pere Oscar La Croix	
The Church and the Socio-Economic Situation in Guadeloupe	35
Pere Serge Plaucoste	
The Netherlands Antilles	39
David Mitchell	
Surinam	43
David Mitchell	
The U.S.A. and the Caribbean	46
David Mitchell	
The Dominican Republic	52
David Mitchell	
Haiti	56
David Mitchell	
Puerto Rico	60
Ivan Meléndez-Acosta	
Cuba	67
David Mitchell	
The Caribbean and Canada	71
David Mitchell	
Part Two — A Look at the Caribbean Economy	77
A Look at the Caribbean Economy	78
David Mitchell	
Plantation Agriculture in the Caribbean	82
based on a paper by Carol Keller	
Tourism in the Caribbean	85
Neville Linton	
The Caribbean Bauxite Industry	89
Anthony Gonzales	

Part Three — The Changing Face of the Caribbean	**93**
Society and Its Tensions	**95**
Irene Hawkins	
Education and Its Imbalances	**101**
Irene Hawkins	
Part Four — Voices in Culture and Religion	**105**
Struggling to Be	**107**
William W. Watty	
The Many Faces of Jamaica	**110**
Alfred C. Reid	
Youth: The Crescent Grows at the Margins	**114**
Oscar Allen	
Summary Report of a 1976 Visit to Cuba	**118**
Jimmy Tucker	
Voices from the Church in Cuba	**123**
Sergio Arce-Martinez	
Part Five — The Caribbean Churches and the Way Forward	**127**
The Religious Spectrum in the Caribbean	**129**
David Mitchell	
The Story of the Caribbean Conference of Churches	**134**
Kortright Davis	
A Perspective: Where Do We Go From Here?	**139**
David Mitchell	
About the Contributors	**143**

foreword

If you find that this book is something of a bewildering mixture. that will be an indication that we are indeed getting through to you. Our Caribbean is indeed a complex area. Because of this we have omitted much that some people would have liked to see included. Others would take issue with what we have included. "This is not the Caribbean as we know it from our travels," some might tend to think about the rich mixture offered to your various tastes.

Obviously we could not, within the limits of a single book, cover adequately the whole range of Caribbean experience. Some of our readers will have travelled within the area and will have become familiar with countries and peoples not mentioned in this book. For example, the many English-speaking islands in the Eastern Caribbean stretching from the U.S. Virgin Islands to Trinidad have come in for no mention. Also omitted are Antigua, St. Kitts and Monserrat, Barbados, the Carnival of Trinidad, the Buccoo Reef of Tobago and the Bahamas Islands, which together make up one-third of the English-speaking Caribbean.

Many North American visitors will have been attracted by one or many aspects of Caribbean life, and may be disappointed by the omission of these particular interests, whether they be the role and status of women, youth, the family, the growing incidence of unemployment, the nature of the welfare services, the wealth of folk culture (calypso songs, reggae music, limbo dancing, Indian festivals, Caribbean theatre, literature, sculpture, painting), or even the exotic nature of Caribbean handcrafts, foods and drinks.

Little has been said pertaining to the place and the needs of the minority groups and cultures. Guyana is now home for a majority of the East Indian population, descendants of immigrants from India who have refined their Hindu faith; Trinidad's East Indians also form a very substantial minority. Yet their cultural customs, language and religion are treated as a minority culture and do not dominate the country. The original Amerindian inhabitants—descendants of the Caribs who dominated the scene when Columbus opened the region to Spanish conquest —now are reduced to small pockets living in St. Vincent, Dominica, Trinidad, Belize, Guyana and Surinam. And in Guyana the integration of the Amerindians into the wider modern community poses problems for the survival of their customs, crafts and communal life, and the ownership of land. Because of the constant change of European control in the eighteenth and early nineteenth centuries pockets of African-French, African-Spanish and African-English minority groups exist in valleys, forest and mountain districts of the region. They maintain distinctive customs, dialects, practices, cuisines. But they are often regarded as second-class citizens, and their culture, crafts and dialects are seen as abnormalities. Very little has been said about the issues facing such a mixed pluralistic grouping of societies as is found in so many Caribbean countries.

Nor have we dealt with the question of migration. Of all the Third World regions, the Caribbean has sent the most sizeable pockets of emigrants to the Atlantic seaboard of the U.S.A. and to the provinces of Canada.

Many North American denominations have made sizeable contributions of money and personnel as part of their missionary work in the Caribbean region. Even today they seek to maintain fraternal relations and relevant forms of witness and mission. But this book does not deal with this contemporary Christian concern or delve into the strengths and weaknesses of this historic association. Nor has anything been said about the training of indigenous pastors and priests, of women workers, deaconesses and nuns, either in the region or in North America. Yet these associations and changes have had some significant influence on the Caribbean Crescent.

There are some gaps in the story—we have ignored some of the significant "trees" so as to be able to view the whole "forest". But this seeming dilemma only highlights the rich complexity of the region. Moreover, we recognize that some of these gaps are filled in in other materials related to the study of the Caribbean Crescent (listed on the back cover).

We wish to thank the many persons across the scattered Caribbean area for the cooperation and action which has resulted in this book.

We hope this book will help the people of North America to understand us, their neighbours, in the Caribbean Crescent to the South.

David Mitchell
Barbados
January, 1977

introduction
A Flight into Eden?

The Caribbean, seen from the air on a fine day, is a model tourists' paradise. Blue seas, white sands, coral reefs, towering forest-clad mountains, rushing streams, lush tropical vegetation, exotic flowers and shrubs invite travellers from both sides of the North Atlantic to escape from the harsh realities of their metropolitan worlds. Yet such escapism often blinds tourists to the accelerating disintegration of the Caribbean's charm and serenity and to the increasing impoverishment of its peoples, despite all efforts made within traditional frameworks of government and society to save it.

Travellers who stay within the customary orbit of airport, taxi, hotel, nightclub, in-bond shop, casino, white sand, cool bar, taxi and airport also miss the rich variety of culture, cuisine, personalities, folklore, art and music which have evolved over the years, hidden from the disdainful eyes of white visitors who have for so long despised the region's "local life."

Rare and fortunate are those from overseas who can share with the local people the wealth of sensation and feeling that makes up the Caribbean, appreciate its native culture, enjoy and respect its inner life, and partake of its people's aspirations for the well-being of their "new race."

The 7,000 odd islands and reefs and the mainland countries that make up the Caribbean Crescent entered written Western history when Columbus landed on one of the Bahama Islands and planted the Spanish flag to the strains of a Latin "Te Deum." His belief that he had reached the "back door" of India by sailing west led the islands to be called the West Indies. The olive-skinned "Indians" who peered through the forests and shrubbery of the beaches at the white-skinned men from the great canoes were the peaceable Arawaks or the fierce Caribs and Ciboney. The peoples of various races, colors and languages who later settled the islands are known as West Indians. Those who went on to settle the shores of the continent, and who have been subject to the same political, social, economic, cultural and linguistic influences, are not called West Indians, since they are not on the island chain, but are included in the wider term "Caribbean peoples", which also applies to inhabitants of Guyana, Surinam, Guyane Francaise (Cayenne)[1] and the Bahamas, even though their countries are not on or in the Caribbean sea.

Caribbean territories first served European nations as military outposts and naval bases guarding routes to the American continents, from which the gold, silver and precious stones of the "New World" flowed eastward into the rapacious hands of Europeans. Every Caribbean country has its ruined stone fortifications, and derelict windmills testify to the wealth that massive sugar plantations tore from the soil after the fever of gold-mining had passed. The original "West Indians" all perished in brutal forced labor, and in the plantation era masses of new manpower had to be imported -- Africans from the West Coast of Africa, Indians from the hinterlands beyond Bombay, Calcutta and Madras, Chinese from Shanghai, Canton and Hong Kong, Portuguese from Madeira, "Syrians" from the Middle East, Indonesians from Java, and Europeans from the Protestant north of the British Isles and Holland and the Roman Catholic Mediterranean south.

Spain's European neighbors did not leave her long in unchallenged enjoyment of the wealth that began to pour back from the New World. Soon Holland, Britain, France and a few small North European countries sent ships and soldiers to claim shares and followed them with settlers and slaves to drag yet more wealth home from the rich soils of their new Caribbean settlements. For three hundred years the tides of conquest, stirred up by European conflicts, swept our islands and continental shores.

Today Spanish, English, French and Dutch are the languages of various Caribbean peoples, whose countries remain tied as by umbilical cords[2] through their economics and trading systems to their European or North American "home countries" (to use a local phrase) or, as they are also called, "metropoles."

The educational systems of the metropoles have been imposed on the Caribbean, to the complete disregard of the more ancient systems of Africa, India, Indonesia and China. The music, art, languages, diets, religions and cultural institutions of these parts of the world have also been despised and suppressed through the centuries by the European exploiters who imposed their rule, economies and cultures on the area.

(1) The three Guianas, once known as British, Dutch and French Guiana, now are called Guyana, Surinam and Guyane Francaise (Cayenne).

(2) *Umbilical cords,* implying that the metropolitan origin and orientation of Caribbean countries controls, and even fashions them, as a mother does a child.

Caribbean economies were deliberately designed to pour cheap raw materials into the expanding industries of Europe. After four centuries, European and North American corporations still ensure that the agricultural and mineral wealth of the Caribbean flows cheaply "homeward" to maintain their industries and manufactures.

Developing countries, including those in the Caribbean, fear that a U.S. government proposal for a "stockpile of primary products" made at the Fourth United Nations Conference on Trade and Development (UNCTAD) at Nairobi in May, 1976, is an attempt to control the prices of their products, while they are obliged to buy the manufactured products of developed countries at any price the latter may demand.

The industrial and communications technologies, the mass media advertising and propaganda that flood in from the North Atlantic now press relentlessly against indigenous Caribbean cultures, attempting to mould the Caribbean peoples into imitative consumers of the manufactures, styles, artifacts, customs, art, music, values and attitudes of industrialized "concrete-jungle" civilization, to con them into buying the North's industrial output and subsidizing its economic system. Many young Caribbeans have been brainwashed by movies, radio, television, and the visits of impresarios into preferring "rock" and "soul" music to calypso, just as their parents were brainwashed into rejecting Caribbean folk songs in favor of "classical" music. Modes of dress, styles of cuisine, types of housing and transport -- all are "Westernized," to the detriment and potential destruction of that which has evolved over four hundred years to suit the Caribbean's climate, resources, needs.

The damage to the Caribbean self-image has been incalculable. Some speak of "going home" when they can save enough for vacations to Europe, while visits to Africa, India or China are merely visits to forebears' birthplaces. People of African descent are the most numerous in the Caribbean, but unlike those of European, Indian or Chinese descent, they were prevented from bringing their languages, customs, family and communal relationships with them. They were dispersed up and down the islands for fear of slave uprisings, and the men were forbidden to practice their paternal functions of fighting, hunting, trading and rearing their families. It is therefore among blacks that the search for identity is keenest, and we hear of "Afro-Saxons," of "black skins, white masks," meaning those who have turned from their African heritages to imitate Europeans and remain forever subservient.

The miscegenation, the cross-cultural pollination, the resiliency and vitality that have produced the modern West Indian or Caribbean person, may offer hope that the present generation will resist the destructive pressures we have cited. It is our hope that this book will help our North American friends know us better and encourage them, in the name of Christ, to stoop with us to lift our burdens. By informed lobbying of their own governments they can enable us to breathe more freely, act responsibly in more genuine freedom, and bridge the widening chasm that commits so many of our people to increasing poverty, growing unemployment and ultimate rebellion.

We hope that what we say in this book will lift the curtain of misconception which lack of information, misinformation, and deceptive tourist-propaganda images have thrown around us, and give you a faithful perception of our situation.

part 1

the colonial legacy

THE COLONIAL LEGACY

Despite the Caribbean crescent's bewildering variety of political systems, races, languages, creeds, cultures and customs, Caribbean peoples all have one thing in common: histories of colonial and neo-colonial domination by European and North American powers. Except for Cuba, treated briefly below but not covered by most generalizations about the contemporary Caribbean,* each country in the crescent has a legacy of control by foreign nations which has continued, with new twists and turnings but no major breaks, up to the present.

Ongoing "metropolitan domination" is of vital, even overriding significance to this volume's contributors in their attempts to define a new mission for a new people. Our Caribbean voices themselves have therefore declared in unison that we should first group and study their countries in light of their relationships to those North Atlantic "metropoles" which now hold predominant influence over them: England, France, the Netherlands and the U.S.A. (with which Canada is increasingly identified in our minds).

Spain was, of course, the first and most important early colonizer of the Caribbean islands and the mainlands beyond. But Spain began to lose ground to Britain in the 17th century, and the last bastions of its Caribbean empire, along with its remaining influence in the region, fell to the U.S. following the Spanish-American War of 1898.

This book's first part therefore begins with "The British Empire," an overview of British hegemony in the Caribbean, followed by more intimate treatments of Guyana and Belize -- little-known and little-studied -- which occupy sections of the mainland at the southern and northern ends of the crescent respectively.

---

*For concentration on Cuba, see *Cuba: People - Questions*, in the series, "People and Systems" (General editor, Ward L. Kaiser, Friendship Press, 1975).

13 The Colonial Legacy

Next comes assessment of the French presence, which is now limited to Martinique and Guadeloupe (along with several tiny adjacent islands in the Eastern Caribbean) and French Guiana Cayenne, a small slice of the South American mainland on the northern border of Brazil.

Haiti, on the western end of Hispaniola, was an early French colony. But mulatto freedmen and black slaves there revolted against Napoleonic France, defying even an army dispatched by Napoleon under his brother-in-law, General Leclerc, and won their independence in 1803. Haiti's later history, as part of the southern border zone of the U.S. however, compels us to study this, the poorest country in the Western Hemisphere, along with Spain's former Caribbean colonies under "The U.S.A. and the Caribbean."

French Guiana lost much of its population, planters and slaves alike, in the devastating cholera epidemic of the 1850s and never regained colonial or historical significance. Shortly after the epidemic it became a penal settlement where France's most desperate criminals were shipped to endure (or perish) on the notorious living hell of Devil's Island. The penal colony was finally abolished in 1946, and since then French Guiana has been used almost solely by France as a space research station.

Our examination of the contemporary French presence in the Caribbean therefore consists of a pair of essays on Martinique and Guadeloupe.

Rounding off our survey of European predominance in the Caribbean are articles on the Netherlands Antilles, six former island trading posts which remain part of Holland, and Surinam, a South American mainland territory which seceded from the Tripartite Kingdom of the Netherlands in November of 1975 to become an independent republic.

Turning finally toward North America, we first trace the general emergence of the U.S.A. primarily as heir to Spain's dominions in "The U.S.A. and the Caribbean" and then focus more narrowly on case studies of the Dominican Republic, Haiti, Puerto Rico and Cuba.

The contrast between the latter two cases is particularly striking. Puerto Rico is now politically torn between becoming a U.S. state, continuing its current status as a "Free Associated State" of the U.S., and attempting to gain its independence. Cuba, whose revolution ousted a U.S.-supported dictator in 1959 and subsequently led to nationalization of U.S. financial interests, is still economically blockaded by the U.S.

In recent history the faces of Caribbean domination have changed. Outright colonial ownership of Caribbean territories has gone out of fashion. As the mechanisms of foreign control over Caribbean economies, resources and politics have adjusted to ensure that rich, developed metropoles still get richer and more developed at the Caribbean's expense, much of the old European center of economic gravity has made the pilgrimage across the Atlantic to North America. "Investments" have become the medium of foreign -- largely U.S. -- domination, backed up by political manipulation. Military force is a last resort for "protecting investments." By these mechanisms the U.S., in the aftermath of the Monroe Doctrine, has extended its economic control virtually throughout the region.

The U.S., however, does not stand alone as North American heir to the exploitation of Caribbean peoples. "The Caribbean and Canada," the final essay in this section, examines the special historical and economic relations between Canada, which has never held any Caribbean colonies, and the British West Indies -- relations which have led toward the emergence of Canada as a "medium-sized imperial power" in the Caribbean and junior partner to the U.S.

THE BRITISH EMPIRE

David Mitchell

After more than three hundred years of conflict between European powers for the control of the wealth of Latin America, Britain emerged victorious. Spain's ring of fortresses in Cuba, Puerto Rico and the seaports of the mainland were powerless against the British fleet with its major bases in Jamaica and Antigua.

Britain had begun the conflict by seizing large continental land masses unoccupied by Spain -- Virginia and the Carolinas to the north, and Guyana to the south. Barbados was annexed in 1625 as a provisioning port for ships destined for Guyana. From 1492 to the 1630s the fierce meat-eating Carib tribes had discouraged settlement in the islands of the Caribbean crescent—no mean feat considering their resources and weapons compared with those of the Europeans, as Elsie Payne points out.[1]

Eventually the British ousted the other European countries -- France, Spain and Holland—and by the first decade of the nineteenth century controlled countries whose languages and laws had been basically French (Dominica, St. Lucia, St. Vincent and Grenada), Spanish (Trinidad) or Dutch (Guyana). Trinidad was then a largely empty country of impoverished Spanish farmers and French-speaking estate-owners, refugees from Haiti and Santo Domingo, along with their slaves.

The first settlements were organized by syndicates whose European colonists, primarily small farmers, planted tobacco, pineapples and cotton, and gathered dye-woods.[2] But in about 1640 the Dutch lost

---

(1) Elsie Payne, "The History of the West Indies," Caribbean Background III, (mimeo), Barbados: Center for Multi-Racial Studies, 1971, p. 35.

(2) *Syndicates*. Grants of lands or of islands were made by European governments to noblemen or groups of wealthy merchants, who proceded to gather bands of settlers and send them out to start settlements and farms.

their settlements in South America.[3] Their commerce was in the hands of Jews who had fled from persecution in Catholic Mediterranean Europe. These traders introduced the cultivation of sugar cane into the Caribbean from Brazil, in line with an overall plan to fill their ships with African slaves for sale in the Caribbean, then with Caribbean sugar for sale in Europe. Their ships also brought machinery needed for the new industry to the Caribbean.

The sugar industry transformed the population of the Caribbean. Between 1650 and 1700 the British and French colonies in the Eastern Caribbean became predominantly African. Jamaica and Haiti followed between 1700 and 1750.[4] The industry also changed land-holding patterns, and with them lifestyles, as its huge plantations crowded out the small farms of the original settlers. In Barbados, 12,000 small holdings were expropriated and formed into 700 large estates.[5] Three years after sugar was introduced one estate was described thus: "Its buildings were mean, with things only for necessity." But fourteen years later an observer wrote, "The gentry here doth live far better than ours do in England. This island is inhabited with all sorts, with English, French, Dutch, Scots, Irish, Spaniards, they being Jews, with Indians and miserable Negroes born to perpetual slavery, they and their seed."[6] Slavery and racism had taken over.

Attempts to maintain a lower-class white population by the use of indentured laborers and political offenders from Britain did not succeed. These indentured servants were treated as harshly as African slaves by estate managers who sought to squeeze the last ounces of work out of them before their agreements of indenture had expired.

The profits from sugar that poured into the British economy from the West Indian colonies gave sugar interests a great deal of power. By the beginning of the nineteenth century the Industrial Revolution had come to Britain, and people had flocked from villages into the new industrial towns of Manchester and Birmingham. But these towns were

---

(3) *Jews in Dutch settlements.* See Harry Hoetink "The Dutch Caribbean and its Metropoles," *Patterns of Foreign Influence in the Caribbean* (London: Oxford University Press, 1972), pp. 103 ff. Cf. text p. 51.

(4) Sir Philip Sherlock, "The Caribbean—Origins and Perspectives," in 'Caribbean Background III',(Mimeo), Barbados: Center for Multi-Racial Studies, 1971, p. 174.

(5) J.H. Parry and P.M. Sherlock, *A Short History of the West Indies*, (London: Macmillan & Co. Ltd., 1956), p. 67.

(6) Quoted in Elsie Payne, *op. cit.*, p. 38

given no representatives in Parliament, while the emptying villages had been allowed to keep theirs. West Indian planters used their money to buy out these villages and control their votes. A struggle commenced between manufacturers who wanted a free world market in Britain for their new wares and the West Indian planters, who wanted to retain the old closed-shop "protectionist" system, in which Britain controlled trade with its colonies and gave preferential treatment to its own businesses, to the detriment of foreign countries. Because these foreign countries were limited and disadvantaged in what they could sell in British markets to pay for their purchases of British manufactures, the sales of goods produced in the new British industries were reduced.

In 1807 Britain abolished its slave trade, and in 1832 the passage of the Reform Bill corrected the representation inequalities in Parliament which the West Indian merchants' sugar-based wealth had supported. In the following year slaves were emancipated in the British Empire. Twenty million pounds were given to the planters for the loss of their "property," but nothing was given the slaves to allow them decent starts in their new lives.

The British Government removed the Anglican churches in the Caribbean from the control of the Bishop of London, appointed bishops for Barbados and Jamaica, paid for the appointment of clergy of the Anglican (English) and Presbyterian (Scottish) churches,[7] erected both churches and schools, and paid the salaries of teachers in these denominational schools and also in schools established by the Methodist, Moravian, Baptist and Congregational denominations. The social class system that had arisen during the periods of slavery and emancipation, built on racial lines, excluded African cultural elements and instituted the British language, religion and social organization.[8]

But the exodus of white planters from the colonies,[9] and the increasing numbers of mulatto small estate owners and professionals in the colonial Houses of Assembly, pointed to the ultimate control of the

---

(7) Until disestablishment in the late nineteenth century the British Government had the power of approval of appointments to the Anglican Episcopal sees or dioceses both in Britain and overseas.

(8) Marjorie B. Wesche, 'Place Names as a Reflection of Cultural Change: An Example from the Lesser Antilles', "*Caribbean Studies*," (Puerto Rico: July 1972), p. 75.

(9) E.H. Carter, G.W. Digby, R.N. Murray, *The Story of Our Islands*, (London Thomas Nelson and Sons Ltd., 1975), p. 86.

colonies by their black majorities. It was a threat the British Government had to take seriously. In 1865 peasants in Jamaica revolted against a harsh economic system favoring the planters, after their situations had been aggravated by drought and the collapse of trade with the U.S.A. brought on by the Civil War. The revolt was ruthlessly crushed, and the British Government then pressured the independent colonial Houses of Assembly to surrender their powers to Her Majesty's Government. Only in the Bahamas, Bermuda and Barbados, where substantial numbers of white planters remained to control the economies and political machinery, was autonomous self-government allowed to continue. This development reflected the clear difference in the ways the British treated their white and black colonies. While the British gave the white colonists of Canada and Australia freedom and self-government, they were busily taking away the political freedom of the black inhabitants of the West Indies, Africa and Asia.[10]

Britain's black Caribbean colonies now found themselves ruled under the Crown Colony system, whose form of constitution offended their elites of mulatto middle-class professionals. A British Governor, appointed by the British Colonial Office, ruled with the advice of a Legislative Council composed of British officials (a Colonial Secretary, a Colonial Treasurer, and an Attorney General) and a group of "Nominated Members" selected by the Governor from among white or mulatto trusted citizens. Later, literate property owners and salaried persons above a certain level were allowed to elect a limited number of Council Members. These Elected Members were, however, always outnumbered by the officials and Nominated Members.

This situation continued into the middle of the twentieth century. In 1937 serious riots in Trinidad, Jamaica, St. Kitts and elsewhere led to a Royal Commission of Enquiry, which exposed the devastating economic and political plight of the region. Although the Second World War intervened and the report was not published until its end, some of its recommendations were implemented during the conflict. In the closing years of the war internal self-government on an adult franchise basis was granted in Jamaica, and was later extended to the other colonies. A system of ministers responsible to a Cabinet under a Chief Minister or Premier was instituted.

The 1937 riots had also led to the formation of labor unions, which

---

(10) Walter Rodney, *The Groundings With My Brothers*, (London: Bogle L'Ouverture Publications, 1969), p. 27.

provided bases for some of the new political parties. In addition, they came together on a Caribbean-wide basis and urged federation.

The Federation of the West Indies, comprising most of the English-speaking Caribbean Islands came into being in 1958. The leaders of the governments of the larger islands formed the Federal Labour Party, while the opposition parties formed the Democratic Labour Party. As the best leaders of the Federal Labour Party remained in the territorial governments, however, the Federal Government was denied the political skills of the region.[11] And the majroity of the Federal House seats of Jamaica and Trinidad (the largest bloc in the House) fell to the opposition parties in these territories, whose Federal Labour Party Governments found themselves represented in the Federation by their political opponents. But for a time the small territories enabled the Federal Labour Party to run the Government.

Eventually, however, the problems of inadequate representation of the large territories, unreasonable apportioning of the Federal budget, inadequate inter-territorial shipping services, lack of Federal power to implement overall economic planning, and inter-territorial squabbles led to the collapse of the Federation in 1962. The Bahamas and the mainland countries, Belize (formerly British Honduras) and Guyana, had remained outside the Federation at any rate. Since its collapse the English-speaking Caribbean countries have been proceeding toward independence separately.

But efforts at regional cooperation have continued in other areas; for instance, in the sharing of regional institutions such as the Federal Shipping Service, the University, meteorological services, and the Caribbean Development Bank. A Heads of Government Conference allows regional decisions on important issues, and a Free Trade Association has evolved into a Caribbean Community (CARICOM) with a Secretariat centered in Guyana, which Belize, Guyana and the Bahamas have entered.

Our governments now work amid increasing international pressure, world inflation, the fuel crisis, balance of payments problems, continuing exploitation of Caribbean resources by foreign investors and multinational corporations, increasing populations, unemployment, diminishing emigration, and decreasing tourism (because of world inflation). They struggle with problems of cooperation, integration, regionalism, and, ultimately, survival.

---

(11) Sir Harold Mitchell, *Caribbean Patterns*, (Edinburgh: W & R Chambers Ltd., 1967). pp. 114-127.

GUYANA

P. I. Gomes

In 1498 Christopher Columbus sailed along a part of the northern coast of South America that later became known as the Guianas -- in the language of the Amerindians who lived there long before the time of Columbus, "the land of many waters"; of majestic rivers at first thought by the Europeans to convey the commerce and trade of inland inhabitants to neighboring regions. But how could there be such great rivers without great towns of wealthy merchants and traders?

With the recognition that an unknown land had interrupted the explorers' westward passage to India came rumors and myths of El Dorado, a city of gold-paved streets and unsurpassed wealth. The quest for it brought conquistadores who plundered and destroyed the riches of this new world. They possessed a determination and greed which, even to this day, motivates the control and exploitation of other people's resources and labor in the name of God or Country or both.

Spanish ships carrying the treasures of Mexico and Peru "homeward" were attacked by pirates of other European nations, and the Portuguese, the English, French and Dutch made attempts to settle on lands Spain had conquered. By 1580 Portuguese traders had built a fort on Guyana's Essequibo River to protect their removal of gold and precious stones, cotton and dyes of the native Indians, mainly Arawaks.

The English adventurer, Sir Walter Raleigh, made a voyage to Guyana around 1595. But, disappointed at not finding El Dorado on the coast, he did not think it worthwhile to found a permanent English settlement there.

In later years, as the quest for gold subsided, the adventurer-robber gave way to another kind of European exploiter. The quest for land, and with it the cultivation of indigo, sugar, cotton, coffee and cocoa, then in great demand in the markets of Europe, brought settler-colonizers to Guyana.

The Colonial Legacy

By 1630 there was a Dutch settlement, New Amsterdam, at the mouth of the Berbice River in eastern Guyana -- the base for a sugar empire. But cheap labor had to be imported before the plantation system could be implemented on the large coastal expanses of rich land. Slaves were brought from Africa and indentured workers from India.

By 1773 the Dutch had established three colonies, spanning the territory's total area of 83,000 square miles, and taking the names of Guyana's three great rivers—the Essequibo, the Demerara, and the Berbice. For some forty years afterward, rivalry between the Dutch, British, French and Spanish for possession of this territory constantly disrupted attempts to organize and expand the cultivation of indigo, cotton, sugar, coffee and cocoa. By 1831, however, the superior might of the British had proved itself, and the territories were unified to become British Guiana, which remained a British colony until formal independence was granted in 1966 and Guyana became a sovereign member of the United Nations. A little less than four years later, in 1970, Guyana became a Co-operative Republic in the British Commonwealth.

Today Guyana's economy is dependent on world-market prices for sugar, bauxite (aluminum ore) and alumina, (partically processed bauxite) and it faces problems similar to those of other ex-colonies.

Contrary to popular myths, Guyana's economic under-development did not occur because Guyanese were lazy, nor because the country has had a small proportion of university graduates, nor because the tropical climate is too overpowering for hard work or modern agriculture. Even more absurd are the myths that the low standard of living to which the great majority of Guyanese are subject has come about because of its large proportion of Hindus and Muslims, or because of the pronounced cultural differences between Indo-Guyanese and Afro-Guyanese, its two major ethnic groups. It is disastrous that one still finds these kinds of "reasons" given in books about Guyana. We must look elsewhere to explain the country's present economic, social, cultural and political condition.

Guyana's past made it a colonial "plantation society," part of what we might call the "back yard" of the British Empire and its capitalistic economic system. A colony is easily understood as an outpost of an imperial metropolitan country whose objective is to control and govern the colonial people and their resources to produce the wealth from agriculture or minerals which the metropolitan country needs to expand its own industries. Historically, however, a plantation society was always more than an economic system of agricultural production. A well-known American sociologist has said,

> ...it was a socio-cultural system in which the lives of white masters and colored slaves...became enmeshed in a system of social relationships...It was on the plantations that the spirit of white paternalism took root...

Until the emancipation of Guyana's slaves in 1838, a few whites -- plantation owners and colonial administrators -- totally controlled Guyana's masses of black slaves, who had been torn out of societies which, in earlier historical periods, had seen highly civilized kingdoms in Western Africa. But slavery had robbed them of their cultural heritages, especially their family structures and religious beliefs.

After 1838 many Guyanese of African descent moved toward acquiring their own land in rural communities and villages being established along the coast, usually near the big sugar plantations, where some found work as agricultural laborers and skilled craftsmen. But they formed an insufficient and unstable labor supply for the plantations, and could not be forced into working for unjust wages. So from the mid-1830s to 1917, plantation owners imported indentured workers from India, Ireland, Germany and China, and Portuguese from Madeira. These were contracted to work for specific periods, usually five years, after which they were free to return to their own countries or to remain in the colonies, working under new agreements or as independent farmers or small traders.

These immigrations account for the ethnic diversity of present-day Guyana, but under colonial policies they also had severe consequences for the class structure, political progress and economic development of the society. The largest numbers of these immigrants came from India, and the result was a multi-racial society -- Guyana is often referred to as the "land of six peoples" -- which at present is 51% Indo-Guyanese, 31% Afro-Guyanese, 12% mulatto-ethnic, 5% Amerindian, 0.1% Portuguese, with the remainder Chinese, Syrians and Europeans.

The deliberate policy of the British Colonial Office was to maintain separation between ethnic groups and prevent the unification as a social force of all those whom the colonial administrators controlled. As experience had demonstrated in many other parts of the world, a colonial society divided along racial and cultural lines was far more manageable.

The Colonial Legacy

The underlying racism of colonial policy and the differences in people's opportunities for earning livings created a social structure which reflected ethnic differences. For instance, while the great bulk of Afro-Guyanese started off in the 1830s as peasant farmers and agricultural laborers, by 1950 some were in teaching, the civil service, law and medicine, with the remaining majority as urban and industrial proletariat. In the early period small-scale retail trade was in the hands of the Portuguese, joined later by some Indians, Chinese and Syrians. These now make up the majority of the local business class. Indo-Guyanese in urban centers now have significant positions in law, medicine and commerce, but the greater majority work as the agrarian proletariat in sugar-cane industry or as rice farmers, large or small, in the rural districts.

In 1953 the first Guyanese elections based on adult suffrage resulted in a landslide victory for the Marxist-oriented People's Progressive Party (PPP,) led by Dr. Cheddi Jagan. The PPP was representative of both the urban and rural working classes, and of both major ethnic groups.

But Guyana, at the "beachhead" of South America," was considered strategic to the Western Hemisphere, and an independent Marxist or Communist Guyana was not in keeping with the foreign policy interests of Great Britain or the United States. The British Government accused Jagan of being a Communist, threw him out of power, and suspended the Constitution.

Thereafter ideological differences and perhaps quests for personal power contributed to a split in the progressive nationalist movement for independence, and a faction of Dr. Jagan's party was formed in 1955, under L. F. S. Burnham, into the People's National Congress (PNC).

Although Jagan was again successful in the General Elections of 1957 and 1961, he was unable to maintain stability. Bitter violence broke out between Indo- and Afro-Guyanese in 1962-64 -- the result of colonially implanted myths that the two groups were naturally hostile to one another and of neo-colonial political manipulations.

The columnist Drew Pearson claimed in 1964 that the United States C.I.A. and British security forces were behind the violence. The conservative-led TUC[1] engaged in an 80-day strike against the Jagan government, and their strike costs of over $1,000,000 were paid by the CIA through the Guyana representative of Public Service International, with

---

(1) The *conservative-led T.U.C.* The (Trade Union Congress) was led mainly by people of African descent who were opposed to the ruling Indian PPP Party led by Marxist Cheddi Jagan.

the connivance of the British Prime Minister, Colonial Secretary, and head of security of the British Government.

The British Government, on the alleged recommendation of U.S. Secretary of State Dean Rusk, then imposed a form of proportional representation on Guyana. The following General Elections which enabled a coalition to be formed under Burnham, composed of both left- and right-wing parties, to replace the Marxist-oriented Jagan government.

Having consolidated his position by various methods, Burnham now seems to be taking his country into the realm of practical public ownership of resources and means of production. As a co-operative Socialist Republic, Guyana still retains a Prime Minister in its highest political office, with a President as head of state. This follows the same pattern as countries such as India and Ghana, and differs from that of such countries as the U.S. and Venezuela, which are republics.[2]

Now Guyana is facing up to the intense struggle of a "poor" nation in a world of large industrial and technologically advanced societies. The grasp of multi-national corporations on its economy, particularly on its sugar and mining industries, its supplies of fuel, machinery and consumer goods, is powerful and dominant. Its present PNC government has moved toward gaining control of its resources by nationalizing the bauxite industry and the various interests of the giant multi-national Booker Group of Companies.

The past has fashioned a Guyanese society of lingering ethnic mistrust, racism, and social class differences based on greed and acquisitiveness. Its future will not ensure dignity, justice, and civil liberty without a new definition of the human person, what values truly protect human happiness, and what social and economic relations can best prevent exploitation of the many by the few. But many young Guyanese recognize the fundamental importance of these matters. They are the real hope for a humane future in a new Guyana.

---

(2) Indian and Ghanian Presidents are heads of state and leave the actual rule to the Prime Ministers: in the U.S. and Venezuela the Presidents are the rulers of their country.

POOR LITTLE BELIZE

Claude Cadogan

From the time I was a small boy some fifty years ago I could hear people saying at times, "poo lee Belize." It was not mock modesty, nor was it complaint. It was, perhaps unfortunately, a kind of resignation to or acceptance of what just seemed to be true. We were poor. We were little -- small in population and insignificant as a part of the British Empire to which, with deep pride, we were glad to feel we belonged.

Looking back on the history of the early years, through the nineteenth century to the first decades of the twentieth, one realizes that Britain treated Belize -- then British Honduras -- just like a warehouse.

Goods of value were here. They were to be had almost for the taking. For the comfort and well-being of those who came to find and take the goods out of the warehouse, homes were build; churches were established, which in turn provided schooling and some cultural pursuits; shopping facilities were provided; a few select clubs were organized and run for the elite who could appreciate them and needed something to make life bearable until they could get back home.

The masses of common people did their best to follow the fashions and "make something of themselves." If life was not too dull, it was not very enterprising: there was a certain quality of peaceful, virtuous law-abiding that made for respectability and drowsiness.

The people of Belize, mostly "Creoles" of that mixed but strongly African race that has been termed "West Indian,"[1] were the labor force

---
(1) *West Indian*. The 'Bay men' were white, coloured and African people who moved from the West Indian islands in the seventeenth and eighteenth centuries, at the suppression of piracy and commerce-raiding. They settled in the rivers and creeks of Belize to cut lumber and logwood for exports to Britain. As they had emigrated from the West Indian islands around the Caribbean Sea they were called West Indians.

New Mission For A New People 26

-- the "cutters" of the lumbering industry, by far the country's largest employer. For eight or nine months of the year they lived and worked in the bush, cutting "B.H. mahogany" -- the finest in the world -- with axes and hauling it to the rivers, using oxen at first, and later caterpillar tractors.

When the rainy season came and the rivers flooded the logs were carried down to the sea and trapped by "booms" at the river-mouths, where they were chained into rafts and towed by tugs to be loaded into the holds and onto the decks of the great Liverpool steamers that lay offshore at Belize City. From there the mahogany departed for Britain, to be fashioned into the finest furniture, or whatever would best line the pockets of the lumbering company's British shareholders.

In the days when airplane propellers were made from mahogany, British Honduras supplied all that was needed. In some places propeller blades of B.H. mahogany from World War I fighter planes now serve as memorials. They are memorials of Belize's once seemingly inexhaustible mahogany forests, too, for the great mahogany forests have long since been exhausted.

In the meantime we celebrated the great national holidays of the Empire, waved innumerable miniature Union Jacks, and lustily sang "Rule Britannia." We were fine children of the Empire, rejoicing that on "our" Empire, "the sun never set."

Children went to school, and were actually taught. Many made good; "very good." Illiteracy rates were among the lowest in the whole Caribbean.

But of course no people remain forever placid and complacent, sleepy and unspirited. After the demanding years of World War I and through the aftermath that led to the Great Depression of the late Twenties the people of Belize began to awaken to the fact that they were "poor, little," and to listen to voices that arose among them.

One such voice came from a man known as Bangula. He spoke with a rich, resonant, throaty voice that reached far (without any P.A. system,) and roared out to groups that gathered on the "Battlefield," an open space in the center of town that is now the City Park in Belize City. He sought to show some better thing to his people, who were wearying of the continuing conditions and lifestyles that seemed to be headed nowhere.

World War I veterans returned home and rioted because they had only medals and ribbons to show for their sacrifices, and "poo lee Belize" was still the "same same." The riot was firmly squashed by British sailors and marines.

In the lull that followed a new diversion sprang up. Prohibition in the U.S.A. made bootlegging an exciting "buccaneering" adventure, risky but highly profitable. Belize was an excellent jumping-off base.

That diversion ended with the repeal of Prohibition.

People began travelling, although until the late Thirties, to travel by ship to New Orleans or Jamaica was a bigger undertaking than flying to Moscow or Singapore is today. The people of Belize began to see and understand how "the other side" lived, and to draw comparisons. Bangula had a slogan, "Weh good fo England, good fo Belize" -- by which *he* meant, if England had it Belize should too, because Belize's needs were the same as England's.

In the middle Thirties the tide of trade unionism reached Belize, and a city barber, Tony Soberanis, rallied workers to it through courageous if not very experienced leadership.

World War II came, and loyal Belizeans once more rallied to the cause of the Empire. What "little Belize" contributed can never be ignored or considered cheap or insignificant.

The war years saw the full exploitation of Belize's pine forests and at the end, at long, long last, a purposeful program of reforestation.

The late Forties challenged the masses to get busy and do something for themselves; political and social endeavors were reoriented toward economic development.

The Fifties brought about a quickening of political awareness that was long overdue. Since then there has been increased thinking about, planning for, and anticipation of national independence.

The learning period has been long and slow. Party politics have too often been one-sided, narrow, and too divisive of a people too small in numbers, too underdeveloped in skills, and too circumscribed in experience to overcome such handicaps with ease.

But Belizeans are a people with potential, capable of "matching their hour" in anything once they "move to it." They are a mixed people of many distinct racial groups, but there is an increasing togetherness among them where the country, its national identity and unity, are concerned. The Spanish and Indians and their mixtures, the Belize Creoles, the Caribs of Stann Creek and Toledo, the remnants of the Maya and

Ketchi Indians, the East Indians of Toledo settlement -- the whole hundred-and-thirty-odd thousand of them -- are realizing and insisting that they belong to Belize, and Belize belongs to them.

The new name Belize for the whole country was difficult for some to accept, because they felt the ruling political party, the People's United Party (PUPS,) had proposed it on party lines. But those who held to British Honduras realized that name would have to go as the country's development proceeded toward independence. So now Belize it is, with a new political capital, Belmopan, still a "creeping baby town" some fifty miles inland from Belize City, the old capital and the one large city (with a population of 45,000.)

Development of natural resources is the great task of the moment. Sugar provides a viable and profitable enterprise in the north, and rice has the potential to become just as important, especially in the south. General food production, for export as well as domestic consumption, also has promise. Fishing is an industry already under development, with the export trade in lobsters paying well.

There are, however, two snags to the agricultural development of Belize. The country is far from the major markets of Jamaica and the southern U.S.A., and transport costs at present are so high as to be prohibitive. And the people of Belize, having been "lumber men" for so long, are resistant to farming.

In addition, Belize is underpopulated, but the people fear the possibility of immigrants flooding in, getting the vote, and in time gaining control of the country.

And capital for investment is limited, even though Belize is "the land of opportunity."

Nevertheless, the present mood of the people is generally of determination and high dedication. The government has committed Belize to membership in the Caribbean Community, and expects that CARICOM will aid its economy through its plan for sharing developmental facilities and enterprises among its members. The Government is also committed to Belize's independence within the British Commonwealth, so that it can exercise its privileges and enjoy its rights as a sovereign nation -- and so that not even the gloomiest of pessimists will be able to think, let alone say, "poo lee Belize."

There is, however, one last, highly dangerous obstacle on Belize's road to the fulfillment of these aspirations -- Guatemala's claim to ownership of the country. This old claim has recently been renewed. Guatemala *must give it up*.

Belizeans think the claim is stupid, and that Guatemala's attempts at intimidation are as unfair as they are upsetting to the country. Belizeans hold their land by simple possession after conflict and combat in which their forebears were the victors. Even if some choose to discount the Battle of St. George's Cay, fought on September 10, 1798, from that time on the settlers of the Bay -- the Baymen, as they were called -- and their descendants have flown the Union Jack, independent of other countries of the Central American Isthmus.

Guatemala, on the other hand, won independence from Spain only in 1821, and became a sovereign state long after the "settlement of Belize" had become a British territory.

Whatever Britain and Guatemala may have decided about Belize has no bearing on the continuing possession of the country by those who inherited it from their forefathers -- who were born there, lived, grew old and died there.

Belizeans hold their land by the same rights as Guatemalans hold theirs. Britain has been willing and ready to try the case before the International Court of Justice, but Guatemala has not. So we Belizeans find Guatemala's claims annoying, upsetting, and truly frustrating in our attempts to develop the country and fulfill the needs of the people whose land it has been for 177 years. Our people love Belize -- poor, little, backward, no-account as it may be regarded by others, we love it.

THE FRENCH PRESENCE AND THE CHURCH IN MARTINIQUE AND GUADELOUPE

Pere Oscar La Croix

Martinique and Guadeloupe hold central positions in the Caribbean Crescent's island chain. Martinique (*Madinina*, "the nice flower island") between Dominica and Montserrat-Antigua. They are small islands compared with the larger ones such as Cuba, Jamaica and Trinidad, but they are densely populated at 324,000 each.

Martinique is 425 square miles of hilly and mountainous terrain -- "a crumpled piece of paper" with a volcano, The Montagne Pelee, or Mount Pele, famous for its eruption in 1902.

Guadeloupe, with a total area of 680 square miles, consists of two main islands--Grand Terre, a flat limestone formation, and Basse Terre, mountainous, volcanic, well-watered by numerous rivers, with an active volcano called "The Soufriere." They resemble a pair of butterfly wings, and are separated by a narrow strait. Attached to Guadeloupe are six small "inhabited dependencies." Four of them -- Terre de Haut, Terre de Bas, Desirade and Marie Galante -- are 15 minute flights away from the main islands, and the other two -- Saint Barthelemy and Saint Martin (half French and half Dutch) -- are half an hour away.

Along with Guyane (French Guyana) and Reunion, in the Indian Ocean, Martinique and Guadeloupe are French *Departments d'Outre Mer* (overseas departments) -- politically, parts of France. But to appreciate the hopes and anxieties of their 650,000 inhabitants we must examine them in their overall geographic, historic, economic, cultural and religious settings.

To be acquainted with these islands exclusively through tourist brochures, or even tourism, is merely to think of them as "sunny and sandy lands, bits of Paradise and plots for resting and idleness." But behind the masks of Caribbean sun, smiles and seemingly exuberant and cheerful natures, they conceal grave problems that threaten the present and future of their people.

When Columbus discovered Martinique and Guadeloupe at the end of the fifteenth century, the islands were inhabited by Caribs, who themselves had driven away or exterminated the more peaceful Arawaks. By 1635, however, Europeans were beginning to overcome fierce Carib resistance in the Crescent, and in that year the islands became French possessions. Except for short periods when they fell under British occupation, they remained French colonies until 1946, when they were designated French *departements* and their inhabitants became full French citizens.

The first crops to be grown in the Antilles, including Martinique and Guadeloupe, were spices and tobacco. Sugar cane was introduced at the end of the seventeenth century. With it, in classic colonial fashion, Negro slaves were brought in to provide cheap plantation labor, and the economy was organized to serve the needs of metropolitan France.

Shortly after the abolition of slavery in 1848, families from the coasts of India were imported to ensure adequate labor for the plantations. Today their descendants, who remain attached to some ancestral practices, form an important group, particularly in Guadeloupe (about 20,000). They take their place in a heterogeneous island population of Negroes, Indians, Caribbean-born whites known as "bekes," Syro-Lebanese, metropolitan French whites temporarily assigned to the area, and mulattos and "metis" -- issues of interracial unions. The legacy of slavery is a latent racism diffused throughout the islands.

With a population growth rate that has climbed as high as 30 percent, the inhabitants of Guadeloupe and Martinique have doubled their numbers in the last twenty-five years. Recently, however, the growth rate has dropped to 27 percent under the combined influences of family planning and emigration, while progress in medical care through the application of French social laws has reduced infant mortality and extended life-spans by making normal care available to everyone.

The French presence in Martinique and Guadeloupe is marked in many pervasive ways. The official tongue is French, although Creole, the same "patois" found in Dominica, is also spoken. Education with its certificates and diplomas, books, laws, money, are all French. Fashion models are French and Western, and most cultural intercourse is with France.

Commercial trade is mainly with France; as French departments, the islands are integrated into the European Common Market and the European Economic Community. Sugar is still the most important product with lucrative prices resulting from their unique European Common Market membership. Bananas have been cultivated since 1920, and trade in this crop, which along with its corresponding services is particularly important in Martinique, is also protected.

The islands, however, have no mineral riches. Industry is not developed beyond a few small enterprises for manufacturing raw materials from France or elsewhere -- for example, a refinery in Martinique, a cement factory and a flour mill in Guadeloupe.

But despite all their ties to metropolitan France, Martinique and Guadeloupe have felt stronger and stronger currents of a search for local identity during the past twenty years, and nowadays their political evolution is torn between two influences. One is "integrationist," tending toward an ever-tighter attachment to France in all respects -- education, economics, life-styles, etc (much of the islands' emigration has been to France). The other attempts to heighten indigenous cultural identity as a basis for political identity. Its support naturally derives from Africans and, generally, those who speak the Creole language.

In addition, cultural intercourse between Caribbean English- and French-speaking islands has been emphasized in the past five years, with increased air traffic playing a major role. Despite language barriers and the fact that bilingual people are not numerous in Martinique and Guadeloupe, tours through the Caribbean are becoming more and more frequent, and missions are now organized on the levels of governments and administrative groupings -- a positive step toward mutual acquaintance between the islands.

* * *

The Roman Catholic Church commenced preaching the gospel in Martinique and Guadeloupe with the arrival of the first Europeans, but in a context full of ambiguities and defective conditions, despite the efforts of some missionaries who had no aim other than to evangelize and know the natives. The announcement of the gospel was often bound up with the presence of white European colonizers: the goal was baptizing rather than trying to convert.

Today superstition is still strong. Since almost everyone is baptized, and the church holds a certain unquestioned power, it takes a prominent part in the lives of French-speaking "Antilleans." Native-born priests have been serving for only twenty years; formerly priests were all European. In 1970, however, the Pope named two indigenous Bishops, and nowadays more than half the ministers are native-born.

Very few Christians are met from the Reformation confessions (Anglicans, Lutherans, Methodists and Reformed). On the other hand, many "evangelical" churches have grown up during the past thirty years -- Seventh Day Adventists, Baptists and Jehovah's Witnesses—the last being the most active and proselytizing of all.

Today Christians of these French-speaking islands face difficult problems almost identical to those of Christians throughout the Caribbean. Because the historical church is more a defender of morals, or of law and order, than an announcer of the good news of liberation, and for many other reasons, it has lost much of its attractiveness. It still involves a sort of faith, but it no longer creates enthusiasm. It has become a part of the old furniture, eventually to be destroyed or abandoned.

But the Church knows the crisis common to all contemporary human group institutions; a crisis made more acute since the end of Vatican II. New compulsions of faith see the light of day, along with new concerns about manifestations of faith.

Tensions are evident between different groups of Christians. Yet it is true that several of these groups are active in Martinique and Guadeloupe, and that their actions meet that general human aspiration to a more just and fraternal world -- a world liberated from "modern" fascinations with profit and riches and all that goes with them. The work of these groups leads to conscientization, to development -- and is there not here a distance from "the establishment?"

The actions of Christians as constituted groups are primarily evident in the spheres of education and culture, such as in the training of "the young Christian student" and "the young Christian worker," and in "the marriage preparation center." In other spheres actions are more diffuse, and performed individually by Christians engaged in political, social and economic life.

Recently the principal tasks of Christians in Martinique and Guadeloupe have been:

- Strengthening of a well-informed faith, accounting for itself in the face of atheist opinion. Christians everywhere have Bible meetings and reflect on the gospel.

- Witnessing in current life, especially in fields vital to the future of the islands: economic, social and political. Christians attempt to show that development based on financial well-being *only* is not sufficient for mankind. They are working for social justice through the social struggle. But all these actions are causing a conservative reaction.
- Conscientization for a critical sense, for taking our own futures well into our hands -- combatting mental habits of awaiting assistance which derive from the colonial attitude of laziness and threaten all of us.
- Respecting the Antillean man. Christians -- and the hierarchy as well -- must act for the respect of human dignity.

Among the island dust of the Caribbean crescent the people of two islands, Martinique and Guadeloupe, are reaching a decisive moment in their history. They are searching for "themselves," wondering who they are and who they can become in relation to the peoples of the other islands and their former mother country.

Christians have their parts to play in this pursuit, and are reckoning on the support of other Christians.

THE CHURCH AND THE SOCIO-ECONOMIC SITUATION IN GUADELOUPE

Pere Serge Plaucoste

Although Guadeloupe has been a "legal" province of France since March, 1946, and its colonial status was then formally ended, over the past thirty years the lives of the island's people have continued to depend on decisions made 4,375 miles away by the French government.

Political power on the island is in the hands of a Chief Commissioner appointed by the Republic of France. Locally elected officials -- mayors, general advisors, deputy senators -- have no real power. They serve purely managerial functions, or as administrators of decisions handed down from metropolitan France.

This political situation has serious economic, social and cultural repercussions on a society which, as an aftereffect of French colonial slavery, is stratified into "clans." The clan structure contributes to delaying the island's development behind a facade of deceit which only exacerbates the situation.

The Guadeloupean economy is based primarily on agriculture and the related field of stock-farming, with fishing next in importance. A division of the economy into three major sectors -- primary, secondary and "functionary" -- clarifies the problems facing its development.

Agriculture, the primary sector, is characterized by a land-holding structure in which vast areas of property are in the hands of a small number of owners. Fifty-five percent of Guadeloupe's cultivatable land belongs to five percent of large property owners or industrial companies whose major objective is to extract maximum profits, and who have no concern for the island's development.

Over the past few years agricultural automation has been pushed to the point of out-and-out industrialization, which has led to greater unemployment. Unemployment touches every stratum of the population, but it is most acute among farmworkers. Landless peasants do not benefit from land reform because the policies of the estates are to their detriment and directed toward profitting the businessman.

The emphasis on traditional export crops such as sugar cane and bananas is causing the cultivation of cash crops to diminish, and our markets are flooded with expensive imported staples to make up for the loss of the island's ability to meet the basic needs of its own people. Approximately 50 percent of our meat is imported, along with substantial amounts of fresh, dried and salted fish.

The second economic sector consists of sugar refineries, construction, public works and a variety of smaller industries dependent on primary imports -- Antilles cement, flour-mill works, breweries and soft-drink manufacturers. .

Sugar refining is controlled by large local landowners and French industrial concerns. Here also, in recent years, the drive to increase profits has led to escalating automation and modernization, along with concentration of operations that has dropped the number of factories from 14 to no more than half a dozen. These developments have of course set off new cycles of unemployment, and the creation of new jobs has halted.

The construction industry and public works depend on contracts, through which their work is controlled by French capitalists and foreign multi-national corporations -- Unite, Jardin-Billiard, Colas. These corporations provide finance capital for large construction projects and force smaller local companies into ruin.

Bureaucratic functionaries make up the third economic sector. Guadeloupean bureaucracy is bloated, and it is actually becoming saturated, both in the public sector (the administration and the army) and in the commercial sector, which divides into two main branches -- small businesses, which are in financial difficulty, and commercial monopolies controlling exports and imports. These are, in actual fact, the economic "game preserves" of various owners and industrialists.

Transport, also a factor, is in the hands of two main French enterprises -- Air France and General Trans-Atlantic Company. Tourism is touted as the panacea for the economic problems cited on the primary and secondary levels, but in reality tourism and its profits are for the rich and well-off. Financing of tourism is augmented by American money and largely controlled by French who do not live permanently on the island, but draw seasonal salaries. They offer little work, and then only subordinate positions, to the Guadeloupeans (blacks).

The total economic situation of Guadeloupe, then, has inevitably led to grave social problems. Unemployment is chronic, endemic, and rapidly increasing to staggering proportions: the index is currently approaching 45 percent. With nearly half the active population attempting to find work, many are emigrating to France and other parts of Europe...but obviously this is not a solution of Guadeloupe's problems.

Guadeloupeans who do not have cultivatable land are increasingly lured to the cities. But there, where money is king and those who possess always search for maximum profits, exploitation of the workers at times leads to conditions resembling those of slavery.

In sum, the socio-economic stiuation of Guadeloupe is fragile and precarious. Guadeloupeans labor, or labor to find work, under a type of colonialism which has created a dependent economy developed according to the needs of the metropole. To meet these needs and keep the economy moving necessitates keeping Guadeloupe in a state of total dependence -- political, social and cultural as well as economic -- under a system which promotes increasing unemployment and prevents any real local development. All this is well understood by the French administration, which favors growth in imports but makes no attempt to expand exports.

The government's response to Guadeloupe's socio-economic problems comes in the form of public welfare -- subsidies for Guadeloupeans, who have been conditioned to wait for this exterior help. But nowadays more and more Guadeloupeans are beginning to recognize the sources of their problems -- to analyse, to struggle for a new stature, to invent, to look for solutions, and to attempt to free their small country from its systematic socio-economic oppression.

In the midst of Guadeloupe's acute and increasingly critical problems, the Roman Catholic Church must struggle both with its past and with its present status if it is to play its true role.

A serious analysis of the slave era, colonialsim or the post-colonial period will reveal that the church has seldom played its true role. On the contrary, and on the whole, it has presented itself as a defender of the established order. At times it has also, in order to preserve its advantages and privileges, allowed itself to be used -- and it still allows itself to be used by the political powers, by the colonialists, by the capitalists. It has projected and still projects the face of a rich church on the side of the influential and not of the poor. Today what can we say about its life? How can it accomplish its mission? Is the Church conscious of what is taking place socially and economically, of what kills people?

Our Church has been and still is an importation to Guadeloupe. It was implanted here without effort, and is above all characterized by its cultural life. Its liturgical language is not understood by the majority of the population, and many pastors are not convinced that the church ought to have a Caribbean personality, a Caribbean culture. They will not come to terms with the fact that the West Indian identity is dampened, by Western domination, by the French, that is by themselves.

Guadeloupean Christians are far from being adults in the faith. Their lives in the faith are largely limited to masses, pilgrimages, and being very devout. And for its part, the Church noticeably has little interest in the dynamics of the people's lives.

The renewal brought about by the second Vatican Council, with its search for a larger truthfulness to the gospel, confused many Christians, and in Guadeloupe resulted in the growth of sects such as the Seventh Day Adventists and the Jehovah's Witnesses, which offer more "security" and supply more specific and concrete moral dictates.

Here and there, however, Christians do take their baptism seriously, and live their faith in creative tension with all the socio-economic realities of the country -- they meet in slum areas, they work with Action Groups (Christian Rural Youth Movement, Young Christian Workers).

But on the whole the church remains very conservative; far removed from concrete life and the example of its Lord who identified with the poor and oppressed. Certainly there has been a little progress, and from the new forces which have brought it about we want to generate more strength to actualize the gospel, to involve ourselves in the life and liberation of this country -- in the face of an embryonic disquietude for the future of the Christian faith that still remains.

It is a difficult task, for at times we ourselves suspect that we may be reaching an impasse. But with the "prise de conscience" of mankind and, above all, the reborn hope of Christians and non-Christians alike in the Caribbean region, we may find the will to break with our dependence on the past and take our destiny into our own hands -- to construct a new society so we can also believe in the possibility of a new world.

THE NETHERLANDS ANTILLES

David Mitchell

During the same period in which Sir Walter Raleigh was attempting the first English settlements in Virginia, Dutch-speaking Protestants in the Netherlands were struggling to win independence from Catholic Spain -- and also seeking to increase their wealth by expanding their trade in scarce and exotic raw materials from the tropics of the East. Indies and the Americas.

Dutch conquests in the Caribbean were motivated primarily by demands of military strategy rather than plans to develop tropical agricultural plantations. After Holland won its independence, its Caribbean colonies served as markets for slaves, contraband military supplies and other necessities of the European and American combatants in the frequent wars that swept the area in the seventeenth and eighteenth centuries. These Dutch Caribbean trading posts are now the Netherlands Antilles Federation -- six small islands. Saba, St. Eustatius and Sint Maarten, a tourist resort shared with the French, lie southeast of Puerto Rico; Curacao, Aruba and Bonaire are just off the coast of Venezuela.

The Dutch in St. Eustatius were the first foreign power to recognize the infant American republic in 1776. In 1781 the British responded by ringing the island with a fleet and seizing over 30 million pounds of goods from the island's warehouses and shipping.

St. Eustatius never recovered. The trade in supplies and contraband dwindled to nothing when the Spanish mainland colonies gained their freedom in the 1820s, and could trade directly with their North American neighbors.

But the Netherlands Antilles had given refuge to Portuguese Jewish merchants fleeing from Brazil, who now established branches of their family businesses in the growing commercial centers of Cuba, the

Dominican Republic, St. Thomas, and the newly independent republics in Central America. Acting as bankers, their firms serviced loans for the newly independent countries through their European connections in return for control over custom houses. The purchase of such a concession in the Dominican Republic, backed by U.S. capital, signalled the start of U.S. commercial expansion which led to the occupation of some of these republics by U.S. marines in the nineteenth and twentieth centuries in order to "safeguard U.S. investments."

By the end of the nineteenth century the Netherlands Antilles were in a period of severe economic decline, and hundreds of people emigrated to find work in U.S.-financed sugar and banana plantations, road and rail construction in Cuba and Central American republics.

In the 1870s Curacao's fine natural harbor became a trans-shipment point for large new European steamers unable to use the smaller and shallower mainland ports. The economic relief brought by this development was however, only temporary.[1]

The economy of the Netherlands Antilles was eventually transformed in 1924 by the establishment of Royal Dutch Shell refineries on Aruba, which could accommodate the large ocean-going tankers that could not enter the very shallow waters of the Lake Maracaibo region of Venezuela. People streamed in from the other Dutch islands to meet the new labor needs -- and also from the British colonies, Surinam, the Central American republics, and further afield. Curacao's population quadrupled to 120,000 by 1960. Thirty percent were neither of local descent nor Dutch citizenship.

But automation of the oil refining industry reduced its work-force from 12,000 in 1952 to 5,000 in 1966, and by that year the industry's contribution to the gross national product had declined from 40 percent to 20 percent. Surplus workers were repatriated to their homelands. But today the labor force continues to increase by 2,000 persons annually, and unemployment runs at 20 percent. To provide work for the newcomers to the labor force would require a minimum annual investment of $32.4 million, or 15 percent of the national income.[2]

The islands have no raw materials. Fresh water has to be expensively

---

(1) Harry Hoetink, "The Dutch Caribbean and its Metropolis" in *Patterns of Foreign Influence on the Caribbean*, (London: Oxford University Press, 1972), pp. 103 ff.

(2) Harry Hoetink, *op cit.*, pp. 103 ff.

distilled. Internal markets are small and wages are high. Industrialization does not seem to offer much hope for development. A fertilizer plant in Aruba and the extension of docking facilities in Curacao do not offer many new jobs.

The governments have turned to tourism, and many new hotels have been opened -- but since they are largely backed by American capital, profits will have to be repatriated to the U.S. In addition, food and luxuries for tourists will have to be imported and paid for. Meanwhile, the flourishing free trade of Curacao has been reduced by U.S. government restrictions on what returning tourists may take home. The one hopeful aspect of the picture is a reduction in the birth rate from 2.5 percent to 1 percent.

Historically the settlers in the islands, as Harry Hoetink points out,[3] comprised two "estates": upper- and lower-class Protestants (in addition to a small elite of Jewish merchants and financiers).

Upper-class Protestants comprised the top ranks of government employees, military officers, plantation owners and professionals. They kept aloof from the lower-class Dutch tradesmen, artisans and clerks, and intermarried among themselves or with Dutch newcomers. They remained members of the Dutch Reformed Church as a mark of social distinction, and even maintained Dutch architectural forms, colors, and other symbols of their origins in their tropical homes.

Lower-class Protestants looked to the Venezuelan mainland for marriage partners, and eventually became "latinized" and Roman Catholic. The colored and Negro segments of the population also became Catholic, as neither the Dutch Reformed Church nor the isolated Jews were interested in converts. The absence of large agricultural plantations meant that the worst excesses of slavery were avoided.

The local language is Papiamento, "a Creole language with strong Portuguese overtones."[4] The Netherlands Antilles are unique in the Caribbean in that this vernacular is used by all social groups, and serves to link the Portuguese, the Dutch and the Africans. This situation came about because when Dutchmen from Europe poured into the Antilles during the oil-refining boom, the old Dutch upper-class families resented the newcomers' attitudes of superiority and wanted to defend their own standards against the different ones of the immigrants. They made

---

(3) Harry Hoetink, *op cit.*, pp. 106 ff.

(4) *Ibid.*, p. 107.

common cause with the other social classes, and Papiamento became the symbol of local cohesion and nationalism.

Politically each island has its own government, but they are linked together in a Federation known as the Netherlands Antilles, with the parliament, or *Staten*, in Curacao. In 1954, along with Holland and Surinam, the Federation became part of the Tripartite Kingdom of the Netherlands[5], established by the late Queen Wilhelmina. The Kingdom, which was governed through a Council of Ministers composed of the Dutch Cabinet and two ministers from the Antilles Federation and from Surinam. These ministers have the right to take part in discussions of matters affecting their countries and powers of delay if they consider government decisions are detrimental to their countries. Foreign affairs and defense decisions are made by the Kingdom's Council of Ministers, but in all else the Netherlands Antilles Government is autonomous. With its independence in 1975 Surinam seceded from the Kingdom.

The contrast with U.S. political control over Puerto Rico is very revealing: Puerto Rico's resident Commissioner in Washington can speak in Congress but has no vote, nor is he a member of the President's Cabinet. Unlike Puerto Rico with the U.S. or the West Indian Associated States with the United Kingdom, the government of the Netherlands Antilles can influence metropolitan Dutch policy at the highest levels. Their political position gives them some of the advantages of independence without inflicting on them the heavy financial burden of maintaining costly embassies or diplomatic missions of their own abroad, and without the disadvantage of their being cut off from metropolitan financial sources. As part of the Tripartite Kingdom the Netherlands Antilles Federation has access to the European Common Market. As Sir Harold Mitchell wrote in 1969, "The Netherlands Antilles. . .have politically a far greater measure of independence, both in theory and in practice, that has Puerto Rico in relation to the United States."

In general the six miniscule countries of the Netherlands Antilles now hover uncertainly, with very meagre resources, wishing to cut their links with metropolitan Holland, but unable to survive financially on their own.

---

(5) The Tripartite Kingdom of the Netherlands comprised Holland, Surinam, and the Federation of the Netherlands Antilles. The latter two each had a minister at the Hague, until Surinam withdrew in 1975. The Tripartite Kingdom is described *before* Surinam seceded in 1975.

SURINAM

David Mitchell

Surinam was acquired by Holland in 1667. This extensive territory on the northern border of Brazil developed early into a classic sugar- and timber-plantation colony run by white Dutch estate owners with the labor of African slaves. In 1773, however, a financial crisis in Amsterdam ruined the estate owners, and their plantations were taken over by Dutch companies who sent out administrators. A colored or Creole elite arose to replace the departed white settlers and occupy the leading positions in government and business.

The abolition of slavery in 1863 necessitated the importation of new cheap labor -- as abolition did in so many other areas of the Caribbean Crescent -- and this came to Surinam from China and Madeira, later from India and Indonesia. Meanwhile Negro slaves who had escaped from the coastal plantations into the interior forests had formed a new subculture, now known as the Djuka or "Bush Negroes," the best remnant of African culture in the Western Hemisphere.

Three years after the abolition of slavery Surinam's economy began to suffer when the opening of the Suez Canal brought fierce competition in Dutch markets from the products of Southeast Asia.

Surinam's present population patterns are largely dictated by the fact that the first generation of Hindustani (East Indians, both Hindus and Muslims) immigrant-laborers were dispersed to the country's rural areas, leaving Paramaribo, the capitol and home of half the colony's population, predominantly Creole. From 1940 to 1950 the Hindustani percentage of Paramaribo's population increased only from 11% to 21% while the percentage of Creoles grew from 62% to 69%. Second-generation Asiatics, however, have tended to migrate to the capital since then, and by 1969 were equal in proportion to Creoles there, with Indonesians 15 percent and other groups about 2 percent each.[1]

To this day there is no common language among all the cultures in Surinam. Dutch is the "official language," but the Moravian Church, for example, uses six languages in its work among Creoles, Hindustani, Indonesians, Chinese, Amerindians and Bush Negroes. (The two largest Christian denominations in Surinam are the Roman Catholic Church and the Moravian Church, or Evangelical Brotherhood.)

Like the former British and French Guianas, Surinam is a land of flat, wide coastal plains, thick tropical forests and mountainous terrain in the interior. The population is concentrated on the flat farmlands of the coast, much of which is below high-water level and protected by intricate systems of "polders" -- drainage canals with sluice-gates emptying into tidal rivers. Bridge-building in the soft alluvial mud of the coast is on the whole prohibitively expensive, and cars and trucks must cross most rivers on ferries (motor barges or ships) which dock at floating wooden ramps hinged to the shores. Women of Creole or African descent wear colorful cotton headdresses ("anijesas") instead of traditional Western hats or bonnets. The anijesas, stiffly starched and folded into various intricate patterns, indicate by their differing shapes the moods or kinds of actions and functions their wearers are about to experience.

The Djukas of the interior are still famed for their intricate carvings on wooden stools, chairs, spoons, paddles, etc., and for their straw and basket work.

Surinam's economic future lies in farming and its bauxite resources.[2] All but two of its sugar plantations have been closed down, but rice has taken the place of sugarcane. More than half of Surinam's farms are occupied by skilled East Indian rice-growers, but the introduction of modern planting and harvesting methods has been slow among the traditionally-minded peasant farmers. Harold Mitchell was of the opinion that "encouragement of the trend towards small peasant holdings has resulted in less efficient agriculture."[3] Bananas, coffee and citrus fruits are exported to Holland in significant quantities. The timber industry is handicapped by the small variety of trees and the

---

(1) Harry Hoetink, *op cit.*, pp. 11 ff.

(2) For state of Surinam economy—see Hoetink, *op cit.* pp. 111 ff. and Sir Harold Mitchell pp. 290 ff.

(3) Sir Harold Mitchell, *op cit.*, pp. 290 ff.

limited number commercially exploitable within any one area, which results in high raw-material costs to a plywood factory in Paramaribo.

Surinam's most important natural resource in recent times has been bauxite, which by 1950 made up more than 80 percent of the country's exports. In 1967 Surinam was the world's second largest bauxite producer, with over five million tons. A large hydroelectric dam has been constructed on the Surinam River, along with a generator and an aluminum smelter to process some of the bauxite inside the country. The dam has also improved navigation on the river, provided cheaper electricity for Paramaribo, and holds out possibilities for improved agricultural irrigation.

By 1966 Surinam's exports of alumina (aluminum oxide produced from bauxite and later transformed into aluminum) had reached 345,000 metric tons, and aluminum exports 25,503 metric tons. Since $18 million worth of bauxite produces $75 million worth of alumina and $275 million worth of aluminum,[4] the value to Surinam of local processing would be enormous if the enterprise were owned by the nation or by local business firms, and not by a multi-national corporation which exports the profits after taxes have been paid.

Despite the relative advantages of Surinam compared with other Caribbean countries, Surinamese continued to emigrate to Holland -- an estimated 40,000 by 1970. Dutch policy had left the future open -- neither the "total assimilation" of French policy nor the "attainment of complete independence" of British policy being the aim. In 1975 Surinam became completely independent. It is now a republic, ruled by a president who is chosen by the Parliament, fifteen of whose 39 members are ministers of government.

---

(4) Vide infra, Anthony Gonzales, "The Caribbean Bauxite Industry." p. 89.

THE U.S.A. AND THE CARIBBEAN

David Mitchell

The European empires which in recent centuries have virtually dominated the globe are disappearing. Caribbean countries, like so many other ex-colonies, are gaining independence -- a long drawn-out process that Haiti began in 1803. Yet the nineteenth century saw many emerging Caribbean nations invaded and controlled by armed forces of the United States.

What was it that turned the freedom-loving Republic of 1776 into the oppressive military and economic superpower of 1976? Why have American troops repeatedly invaded the small nations scattered around their country's southern borders? How is it that American officials, guarded by American marines, have moved in to take complete control of the customs departments of independent nations?

Why have the American people gained the reputation of being so materially-minded that only the Almighty Dollar can speak? Why have Caribbean peoples come to distrust Americans and think they are only after the "quick buck" -- and will do *anything* in the world to get it? How have we come to believe that, despite some warm and friendly relations with individual Americans, we can only look forward to more economic bullying and manipulation, encouragement of corruption and dictatorship, and "destabilization" through incitement to riots, revolts, assassinations and invasions by official agencies of the U.S. Government and American private enterprise?

The peoples of the Caribbean are becoming very afraid of the U.S.A.

America began its life as a nation because of its determination to free itself from the same kinds of injustices it now visits on the Caribbean.

Between 1664 and 1774 harsh acts of the British Parliament had hung intolerable economic burdens around the necks of the North American colonies. North America could not trade directly with its

French or Spanish colonial neighbors except by paying heavy tariffs. Foreign goods had to be sent across the Atlantic first to Britain before being imported to North America. Smuggling in times of peace and contraband-running in times of war became an essential feature of American colonial life. Sir Harold Mitchell observes, "The tightening by Great Britain of the Mercantile System undoubtedly contributed to the break with the North American colonies."[1]

With the independence of the thirteen American colonies in 1783 and the U.S. Government's purchase of Mississippi and Florida from Spain in 1821, the infant nation's control of its Atlantic territory was complete. But Great Britain still discriminated against American ships and goods entering her Caribbean colonies to the south, and the raw materials and markets of the tropical countries there were closed to American penetration.

By the time Spain lost her Central and South American colonies at the close of the Napoleonic Wars, however, the power of the United States had grown to the point where Britain proposed that it and the U.S. should jointly announce that no European nation would be allowed to attack or annex any Latin American country. But Secretary of State John Quincy Adams, against supporting British policies, persuaded President James Monroe to deliver a message to Congress on December 2, 1823, unilaterally guaranteeing Latin countries in the Western Hemisphere against European interference "for the purpose of oppressing them, or controlling in any other manner their destiny."

The famous Monroe Doctrine was approved neither by the House of Representatives nor the Senate. For many decades Congress would be looking to the West, and would lead the U.S. into a period of isolationism. In any case, the U.S. Government was not strong enough to enforce the Monroe Doctrine unilaterally, and Britain, Spain and France repeatedly ignored it, as in France's ill-fated attempts to set up empires in Brazil and Mexico during the U.S. Civil War.

At the close of the Civil War, despite continuing Congressional preoccupation with internal domestic expansion, the U.S. Government negotiated with Denmark for purchase of the Virgin Islands, and with the Dominican Republic for the sale or lease of Semana Bay for a U.S. naval base. It even proposed that the Republic itself become a United States territory, with a view to ultimate statehood. But Congress, true

---
(1) Sir Harold Mitchell Bt., *Caribbean Patterns*, (Edinburgh: W. & R Chambers Ltd. 1967), p. 368.

to form, would not approve the proposals: America's energies were now taken up with grabbing the lands of the Indian tribes west of the Mississippi and expanding to the Pacific coast.

When this was done, however, Congress and big business found it in their interests to "discover" the Caribbean. As Professor Louis J. Halle puts it, "A change in our position from an Atlantic coast nation to a continental nation with two ocean fronts to defend suddenly made Central America and the Caribbean an area of vital strategic importance for us."[2]

By the end of the nineteenth century, therefore, the American government was ready to seek a shorter sea route between its east and west coasts and "adequate defences" of its long coastlines. In the Caribbean, the Monroe Doctrine could now be applied.

After investigations of the feasibility of cutting a canal either in Nicaragua or the Panama province of Grand Columbia, the problem of a shorter sea-route was solved when Panama declared its independence in 1903 and agreed to a treaty assigning the Canal Zone to complete U.S. control. (The canal was built with the help of labor from the English-speaking Caribbean countries and opened in 1914.)

But America's problem of "defence" was from the beginning linked with the question of economic spheres of influence. President Theodore Roosevelt's solution was to prevent European nations from using naval force to collect debts from Latin American nations. His Roosevelt Corollary to the Monroe Doctrine stated that only the United States would have the right to intervene in the affairs of any Latin American country to enforce collection of international debts.

Ivan Melendez, tracing the aftermath of the Monroe Doctrine, writes in a recent paper: "The Monroe Doctrine was essentially a Caribbean Doctrine, affirming the vital interest of what it (the U.S.) considered to be its inland sea.

"It was this new policy of intervention that erupted so explosively in the war of 1898 against Spain. Moved by the new spirit of Manifest Destiny, convinced that she must be supreme in the Caribbean, the United States launched a crusade to expel the Spaniards from Cuba and Puerto Rico. Spain, whose authority was already disintegrating, would

---

(2) Louis J. Halle, *American Foreign Policy*, (London: Allen and Unwin, 1960), pp. 163-164.

The Colonial Legacy

be taught a lesson at relatively little cost and the United States would proclaim its role as defender of the Americas.

"A war fever swept your nation. The Press wanted war, the Congress wanted war, and presumably even the people wanted war. Everybody wanted war except the Spaniards, who made things difficult by complying with most of the demands served upon them by Washington. The USS Maine exploded in Havana under mysterious circumstances and a *casus belli* was miraculously furnished.

"The United States Army swarmed across the straits into Cuba, and the last outposts of Spanish authority in the New World were wiped out. Cuba and Puerto Rico were detached from Spain, the latter becoming a colony of the United States and the former, only narrowly escaping annexation, retained its formal independence. Its freedom of manoeuver, however, was sharply limited by the Platt Amendment which was incorporated into the Cuban Constitution and embodied in the 1903 Treaty with the U.S.A. Under the Platt Amendment the United States reserved for herself 'the right to intervene in' Cuban affairs 'for the preservation of Cuban independence (and) the maintenance of government adequate for the protection of life, and individual liberty.'"[3]

Samuel F. Bemis remarks that for the United States, the Platt Amendment marked "an era of protective imperialism focussed on the defence of an Isthmian canal... vital to its naval communications and to its security."[4]

By the end of World War I the Dominican Republic and Cuba had each been invaded three times by U.S. marines, and in 1915 an occupation of Haiti began that was to last for nearly twenty years.

As the twentieth century continued, the United States established bases in Puerto Rico and the Virgin Islands. After the outbreak of World War II the British gave the United States military concessions in their Caribbean colonies in return for the loan of 50 mothballed World War I destroyers. American airfields were built in Bermuda, the Bahamas, Jamaica, Antigua, St. Lucia, Barbados, Trinidad and Guyana, in some cases accompanied by naval bases. Some of these airfields became the airports of developing Caribbean countries in the post-war period.

A fundamental but short-lived change in U.S. foreign policy came

---

(3) Vide infra, Ivan Meléndez, "Puerto Rico," p. 60.

(4) Samuel F. Bemis, *The Latin American Policy of the United States*, (New York: Harcourt, Brace and World, 1943), p. 140.

about with the election of President Franklin D. Roosevelt in 1933. Under his "Good Neighbor Policy" the occupation of Haiti ended, the Platt Amendment was abrogated, and a new era of cooperation with Latin America began.

But the U.S.-Soviet Cold War of the mid-1950s brought fears of Communist infiltration and subversion in Latin America, and with it an end to the Roosevelt policy. A further justification for U.S. intervention in Latin America arose -- one which is still alive and deadly today.

An early and important victim was left-wing President Arbenz of Guatemala, who was surrounded by advisers "suspected to be Communists." Arbenz was threatening to expropriate the huge Guatemalan holdings of the giant United Fruit Company, and had arranged for a shipment of arms from the Communist bloc. In mid-1954 President Eisenhower slipped the leash on the C.I.A. A squadron of planes allegedly sold to the government of neighboring Nicaragua by the U.S. Air Force supported a "rebel" invasion. The victorious rebel leader arrived in the capitol in the U.S. Ambassador's official plane.[5]

U.S. military aggression had recommenced. America's briefly interrupted transformation from oppressed to oppressor was reaffirmed.

Just as British forces landed at Boston in 1775 to protect British capital, trade and customs dues, so American marines have landed in Havana, Port-au-Prince and Santo Domingo in the twentieth century to protect U.S. investments and trade. It is, to the peoples of the Caribbean, bitterly ironic that the same kinds of economic pressures exerted by Britain on the original thirteen colonies of the United States are now ruthlessly exerted by this "great world power" on the small nations that ring the Caribbean basin to its south.

Tight quotas and high import tariffs restrict exports from non-U.S. Caribbean countries to the United States. American and Canadian firms ruthlessly exploit and deplete the natural resources of their southern "neighbors" and put every conceivable obstacle in the way of their turning precious raw materials into manufactured products within their own countries and for the benefit of their own people. Meanwhile North American manufactures freely flood the markets of under-developed countries which have no means of meeting the balance-of-payment deficits this rampant consumerism creates.

---

(5) Mitchell, *op cit.*, p. 376.

The U.S. Government restricts air services to its country by Caribbean airlines and, in a particularly specific echo of 1776, limits shipping service between the U.S. and the Caribbean to subsidiary companies owned by U.S.-based multi-national corporations. In addition, cash and credit are siphoned from the profits of businesses in the Caribbean through branches and subsidiaries of Canadian and U.S. banks.

The investments of U.S. businesses, with the political, economic and social evils they have spawned in the Caribbean, are in the end "guaranteed" by the economic and military might of the United States. It is one of the more regrettable turnings of recent history that we Caribbean peoples are increasingly forced to see the American Government in its own self-created, aggressive and oppressive light.

THE DOMINICAN REPUBLIC

David Mitchell

The Dominican Republic occupies roughly the eastern two-thirds of Hispaniola, which after Cuba -- immediately to its west -- is the largest of the Caribbean islands. Haiti occupies Hispaniola's western end.

The Dominican Republic was the site of the first effective European settlement in the New World. Christopher Columbus left his brothers, Diego and Bartholomew, in charge of it while he went on further voyages of exploration. For many years thereafter, Santo Domingo City was a base from which Spanish expeditions set out to conquer other New World lands: Jamaica, Puerto Rico, Cuba, Florida, Mexico, Peru and other parts of the continent. The oldest university in the New World was founded there in 1538. Diego Columbus's residence in Santo Domingo City has now been restored as a tourist attraction, and Christopher's remains are reputed to have been brought back from Spain and interred in an ornate tomb in the Cathedral.

After an initial exploration throughout the island, the Spaniards abandoned the valleys of the north and west as the more energetic and ambitious of them were drawn away from the pursuit of agricultural wealth by the lures of Mexican and Peruvian gold. French settlers replaced them in the west, and France's control of that part of the island, later known as Haiti, was recognized in 1697.

The less energetic Spaniards who remained in what is now the Dominican Republic were not agriculturally inclined, and the African slave population there never grew to the proportions it reached in Haiti.

Early in the Napoleonic era all Hispaniola came under French control, but a bitter slave-revolt erupted in Haiti. Toussaint L'Ouverture, one of its leaders, attempted to conquer the island's Spanish section, but Napoleon had him kidnapped and taken to imprisonment in France.

The Colonial Legacy

In 1809, after Napoleon had swept over Spain, the Spanish settlers on Hispaniola threw off French rule, and went on to win their independence from Spain in 1821 through a revolt against King Ferdinand VII.

But in 1822 the second mulatto-elite President of Haiti, Jean-Pierre Boyer, invaded Santo Domingo and subjected its people to a harsh rule by Negro Haiti. The university was closed and links were severed with the Roman Catholic Church. As history was to prove with a vengeance, the lighter-skinned Dominicans never forgave the Haitians.

An 1843 civil war in Haiti allowed the Dominicans to regain their independence, but it was independence in name only. Corrupt and ruthless dictators alternated as Presidents. One of them brought the Republic back under the rule of Spain in 1861, and was appointed administrator, with the title of Captain-General. But by 1865 the Republic had regained its independence once more.

In the last years of the century one of the presidents involved the government in fraudulent foreign loans, and European creditors threatened to have their governments seize the custom house to guarantee repayment. This led President Theodore Roosevelt to announce in 1905 that the U.S. Government might be forced to collect debts owed by Latin American governments to prevent "foreign intervention" in the Western Hemisphere. During the administrations of Presidents Taft and Wilson, U.S. Marines did occupy the Dominican Republic. In the latter case they stayed for eight years, until 1924, when an election brought Horacio Vasquey to the Dominican Presidency for another term.[1]

But the U.S. military occupation had laid the groundwork for a greater tyranny: Rafael Trujillo, trained and groomed by the U.S. Marines, head of the nation's police force, seized power as soon as the Marines were gone. He held it, either directly or through puppet Presidents, for the next thirty-one years.

The U.S. military had trained Trujillo to be efficient. He efficiently imposed a vicious control on "his" country. As Sir Harold Mitchell relates, "Enemies of the President were ruthlessly eliminated. While some were imprisoned, others might be found shot in automobiles or would simply disappear." Trujillo's men even went so far as to kidnap one from New York City in 1956 and take him to the Dominican

---
(1) Sir Harold Mitchell, *Caribbean Patterns*, (Edinburgh: W & R Chambers, 1967), pp. 68 ff.

Republic for torture and execution (or he may have been killed aboard ship en route.) In addition, the lingering bitterness toward Haiti erupted with overwhelming brutality when Trujillo ordered the machete massacre of all Haitians in the Republic.

The "Benefactor," as Trujillo arranged to be called, instituted a vast regime of corruption which literally made the Dominican Republic his private domain. At the height of his power he personally owned fifty-seven enterprises accounting for 43 percent of the nation's industry, and much of the remainder was in the hands of his family and other hangers-on. As Sir Harold Mitchell comments, "His title of the 'Benefactor' applied more aptly to the good he did for himself, his family and his friends than to that he did the country."[2]

With his own best interests at heart, Trujillo ruthlessly developed the sugar and tobacco industries while his brothers took control of bananas, charcoal for export, and the prostitution racket. For the benefit of neither the workers nor the people at large, he developed a solid industrial base, extending even to a small-arms factory. By the end of his rule the Dominican Republic was one of the most efficient of the Latin American countries in terms of roads, harbors, airfields, hotels and public buildings.

The Benefactor's infamous brutality, however, led to his downfall. Other O.A.S. countries turned against him; the U.S. withdrew naval and military aid; tourism declined; inflation spiralled; and in 1961 he was finally assassinated.

In 1962 the Republic's first free election in thirty-eight years brought Juan Bosh to the Presidency on a wave of support from both peasants and intellectuals. He was soon ousted, however, under pressure from extreme right- and left-wing factions and amid U.S. fears that he would allow communists to take over the country. When civil war broke out in 1965, President Johnson sent in U.S. troops to protect American investments. The troops were eventually placed under O.A.S. control, and after another election (in which women had also been given the vote) all O.A.S. forces withdrew from the country.

The election of moderate right-wing Joachin Balaguer, who had swept the countryside, was witness to the perpetual U.S. fear lest another power intervene in the Caribbean. Balaguer, a U.S. protege, had served a term as one of Trujillo's presidents. During the period of

---

(2) Harold Mitchell, *op cit.*, p. 68.

the anti-Bash coup, U.S. aid had expanded from $12 million to $130 million, and the American Embassy staff had swelled form 86 American and local personnel to 401 persons. Balaguer, as one of Trujillo's former front-men, is no stranger to physical violence. Recently reports have come that "La Banda," allegedly a group of left-wing men blackmailed and directed by the police, have been involved in political beatings and assassinations.

The Revolution was also a witness to the fact that three decades of tyranny had left the Dominican Republic bereft of the intellectual, civil-service and middle-class leadership necessary to reshape the country's potentially viable economy for the benefit of all and as a tribute to the democratic way of life so lauded in North America. Americans should ask themselves how much of the non-development of the ruins of Spain's Caribbean Empire the U.S. Government has brought about.

HAITI

David Mitchell

Haiti is called "the Pearl of the Antilles." It was the second country in the Americas, after the United States, to win its independence, and the first free Negro state in the modern world.

During the Haitian revolution, however, the factories and irrigation systems of the hated French-owned plantations were destroyed, precipitating a long erosion of Haitian agriculture, and the nation was divided between black ex-slaves in the north and a mulatto "free elite" in the south. For a time there were two governments -- that of the Negro Christophe in the north and that of the mulatto Petion in the south.

The political story of Haiti has continued since on the ruins of a devastated economy, a decayed agriculture, conflicts between blacks and mulattos (including discrimination in favor of the mulatto cultural elite both in local schools and in opportunities for higher education in France,) and a sad history of corruption, personal greed, and political murder and assassination. One writer says, "Unleashed personal ambitions began to make use of those who had learned only to fight wars and who became, unknowingly, mere pieces in the criminal game of a fratricidal struggle... the rural masses were forced from time to time to exchange the cutlass for the gun without knowing why."[1]

At the height of World War I in 1915, Guillaume Sam, at the head of a rural army from the northeast, captured Port-au-Prince. His connivance at the murder of 167 of his enemies, including several leading citizens, roused the fury of an urban mob which forced its way into the French Embassy where he had taken refuge, dragged him into the streets and killed him.

In response to this chaos France sent naval units, and the United States landed troops and forced the Haitian government to sign over

---

(1) Alain Rocourt, "The Challenge of Development in Haiti," in *With Eyes Wide Open*, (Trinidad CADEC, 1971), P. 73.

control of the national finances to them. Ostensibly the Allied powers —Britain and France—were afraid Germany would intervene and establish coaling stations for its commerce raiders. It was hardly ever noted that American financial interests had already gained control of the National Bank of Haiti from French financiers. Since then U.S. business interests have backed dictatorship, gained increasing control of agriculture, tourism, mining, manufacturing and craft industries, and acted to prevent the growth of democracy and of trade unionism.

In 1934 the U.S. restored financial control of Haiti to a national government under President Paul Magloire, a thinly disguised dictator who (as in so many instances -- Santo Domingo, Guatemala, Brazil...) had been trained by the U.S. military mission. His successor, Dr. Francois Duvalier, a black medical doctor well-known to the masses, became a symbol to them of their "victory" over the mulatto elite. But the notorious "Papa Doc," who kept his stranglehold on power through a dreaded paramilitary organization known as the Tonton Macoutes, also became a world-wide symbol of the evils of dictatorship through terrorism. At his death his son Jean-Claude, succeeding him as "President for Life," stays in control while the more dreaded features of his late father's regime are toned down.

In 1973 Haiti presented a picture of grave under-development. Per capita income was $75 per year, the lowest in the Western Hemisphere -- but most of this was concentrated in the hands of the mulatto elite, and the poverty of the masses must be seen to be imagined.

In 1970 Haiti's population stood at 5 million, with a density of 1,398 per square mile of productive land, and at an annual growth rate of about 2.5 percent the population is expected to approach seven million by 1980, with pressure on arable land -- itself in deteriorating condition -- reaching cataclysmic levels.

Haiti's road system is very inadequate. Out of 1,873 miles of main roads, only 10 percent are asphalt or concrete, while 36 percent are surfaced with stone or gravel, and 54 percent are dirt.[2] The country's departments are therefore very isolated from each other. Transport needs can only be met by expensive jeeps.

There has been great resistance by the 2 percent mulatto elite to the use of Creole, the language of the masses (a mixture of African and French with its own form of syntax) in education and religion. The

---

(2) CHISS, "Problems of Social Development in Haiti," *Ibid*, pp. 91, 92.

illiteracy rate in French has been very high -- 86 percent around Port-au-Prince and 92 percent in rural areas.[3] But the use of Creole has been increasing, and through the work of the Methodist mission the Laubach method of literacy training has been initiated. Now a national commission has begun to produce basic literature in Creole. A drawback in rural development, however, is that education in urban areas is the responsibility of the Ministry of Education, while that in rural areas is under the Ministry of Agriculture, which has very limited resources. A reduction of U.S. aid to the Duvalier Government in 1962 led to an 85 percent reduction in the construction and maintenance of rural schools.

There are, however, some positive points and hopeful signs. The absence of a plantation economy breeds a spirit of independence and friendliness. A waiter will tell an absent-minded smoker whose elbows on the table prevent a meal being served, "Sir, you cannot drink a pipe." In a small guest house, a visitor back from a tiring day will be asked by a maid serving his evening meal, "Well, what sort of a day did you have?"

And all across the country the Christian churches are taking up the challenge of development. Bright children from village congregations are given trades and simple teaching skills and sent back to their villages to open private schools and become leaders of the network of small Christian congregations. Agricultural development, reforestation, community cohesion and action, simple crafts and trades, are being furthered in pockets of denominational presence and influence. The absence of a national communications network, however, prevents the development of an overall national thrust.

The resiliency of the rural Haitian character and culture under the adverse conditions that have prevailed for so long must be admired. Voodoo provides a "fatalistic" philosophy that sustains viability when hopes are disappointed. Christian names and forms are sometimes taken over, but the rural black masses have never given themselves to the traditional Christian beliefs of their urban mulatto elite opponents. Dancing, drumming and art forms play more immediate and practical parts in their daily lives than they do in the lives of most Caribbean peoples. An amazing vitality and verve animate Haitian sculpture, wood-carvings, paintings and craft products. Even the sides and backs

---

(3) Sir Harold Mitchell, *Caribbean Patterns*, (Edinburgh: W & R Chambers, 1967), pp. 63, 64.

59 The Colonial Legacy

of country buses are adorned with brightly colored designs which are far more pleasing and edifying than the horrible commercial designs on the billboards and commercial vehicles of Western civilization.

So Haiti preserves an innate consciousness and vitality inside a shell encrusted by decades of non-development and decay, and every day its future raises anew the question -- Is it too late to scrape off the encrustations, to crack the shell, and to see the "Pearl of the Antilles" gleam?

PUERTO RICO

Ivan Meléndez-Acosta

Puerto Rico is the easternmost island-peak of the Greater Antilles, a largely submerged mountain chain that separates the Atlantic Ocean to its north from the Caribbean Sea on its south. It lies about 1,500 miles southeast of New York City, less than three hours away by plane, and is about the size of Long Island -- 100 miles from east to west and 35 miles from north to south.

Unless one includes its centuries of aboriginal Indian occupation, the history of Puerto Rico began on November 19, 1493, when Christopher Columbus landed there and claimed the island for Spain. But Ponce de Leon and his soldiers, who followed in 1508 to conquer the Indians and begin a colony, were Puerto Rico's first foreign settlers.

Negro slaves arrived in Puerto Rico as early as 1513, but other islands, such as Santo Domingo, proved more profitable for development and Ponce de Leon himself departed to discover Florida and die in Cuba. By the time the first English settlers had landed in Virginia and the first pilgrims in Massachusetts, however, European civilization had been established in Puerto Rico for nearly a century.

For nearly 300 years Puerto Rico served Spain chiefly as a strategic military outpost. Its gigantic fortress, El Morro, begun in 1540 and finished three-quarters of a century later, guarded the Caribbean from every hostile fleet. Supported by other fortresses, it repelled Sir Francis Drake and many subsequent invaders.

The growth of the island's population and economy, however, were slow indeed. San Juan, a walled city, contained its coteries of soldiers, priests, politicians and their followers. The rest of the island was almost a separate world -- a thin, rustic residue of farmers ignored by the city.

Not until the nineteenth century did momentous changes sweep the island. Immigrants by the thousands, some of them well-to-do, arrived from nearby countries torn by civil strife. Sugar plantations proliferated, and thousands of slaves were imported to work them. The cities of Mayaguez and Ponce assumed some importance. And the Spanish Crown began to take more interest in the island's welfare and its possibilities for producing agricultural wealth. The island's government remained autocratic, making reluctant concessions in taxes and other privileges to attract settlers and for the most part was indifferent to disease, ignorance and malnutrition.

Yet the population rose to nearly a million, and public interest in civil rights increased with awareness of British, French, and especially American democracy. In 1869 Puerto Rico followed the United States in abolishing slavery, and trade with the U.S. grew apace. A few North American farmers began to establish themselves in the island's coastal areas.

During the nineteenth century Puerto Rican political awareness also began to express itself in movements for independence and autonomy under the Spanish Crown. But the new United States policy of intervention in the Caribbean, announced in the Monroe Doctrine of 1823, eventually led to the Spanish-American War of 1898, and the acquisition of Puerto Rico by the United States.

For more than thirty years after the Spanish-American War, colonialism continued in Puerto Rico with its typical spawns of exploitation: company towns, mechanized mills, huge plantations -- often under absentee ownership -- and grinding poverty for the masses of colonial peoples. Profits were taken overseas by the millions, and those that remained were absorbed by such heavy costs as those of importing the bulk of consumable goods.

Inevitably, the standard of living remained low. In 1929 an average working-class family's weekly wage was $6.47, or twelve cents per person per day. Governors were appointed by U.S. Presidents, and few had either capacity to govern or sympathy with the people of the island. Insular politics were controlled primarily by and for those with vested financial interests. Under such conditions, and despite some nominal self-government, it is hardly surprising that men who earned 10¢ an hour for back-breaking toil in the hot fields and women who earned 3¢ a dozen for hemming handkerchiefs commonly sold their votes for $2.

During the 1930s, however, the Roosevelt administration encouraged the mood for social change in Puerto Rico, and Rexford G. Tugwell, a leading New Dealer, served as a vigorous Governor. And if 1898 was a milestone in the history of Puerto Rico, 1940 was a year of destiny. In that year the Popular Democratic Party, with its slogan of "Bread, Land and Liberty," achieved its first limited success at the polls. Luis Muñoz Marin, Popular Party leader and a strong advocate of socialism, rose from the presidency of the Senate to become the first Governor elected by the people. Marin's party is responsible for Puerto Rico's current status as a Free Associated State, or Commonwealth. Under this status the benefits of free trade continue, so that sugar, particularly, can enter the U.S. market without ruinous tariff barriers.

Although Puerto Ricans have been United States citizens since 1917, they cannot vote for the President of the U.S., and have no representation in either the Senate or the House. Their Resident Commissioner in Washington may speak in the House of Representatives, but has no vote.

Puerto Ricans do not pay U.S. federal income taxes. The Commonwealth treasury retains all excise taxes on rum and other local products.

At the same time, federal services are allocated to Puerto Rico on terms often similar to those for American States. Young Puerto Ricans, however, were subject to the United States Army draft, even though they did not (and still do not) have a direct legal voice in determining U.S. military and foreign policy.

The Commonwealth of Puerto Rico has its own constitution, adopted in 1952. Under it an elected legislature passes all Puerto Rican laws and provides for their enforcement. These laws are, however, subject to review by U.S. federal courts, as with any state of the Union.

The establishment of Puerto Rico as a Free Associated State in 1952 was hailed by the architects of the arrangement as the end of Puerto Rico's colonial relation to the U.S. This view was affirmed by the Eighth Session of the General Assembly of the United Nations in 1973 when it accepted the position of the United States delegation that Puerto Rico's status constituted the attainment of what the charter calls "a full measure of self-government."

Nevertheless, advocates of U.S. statehood for Puerto Rico as well as proponents of Puerto Rican independence have continued to argue that the current Commonwealth or Free Associated State status of Puerto Rico is merely a camouflage for the island's neo-colonial exploitation by the U.S. Pro-independence groups have petitioned various organs of the United Nations, most notably the General Assembly's Special Committee on Colonialism, for a review of Puerto Rico's case and the restoration of the country to the UN's list of territories covered by

Chapter XI of the Charter and the 1960 Declaration of the Granting of Independence to Colonial Countries and Peoples. (Resolution 1514, XV; of December 14, 1960.)

The U.S. Government does have exclusive jurisdiction over Puerto Rico in such matters as citizenship, foreign relations, defense, immigration and emigration, foreign commerce, currency, maritime and air transportation, postal services, radio and television. Furthermore, the U.S. exercises total or partial control over wages, labor-management relations, environmental contamination and pollution, internal transportation, public health, quality standards for food and pharmaceutical products, bankruptcy proceedings, rights of eminent domain over land and other properties, and banking and loan organizations.

The defenders of Commonwealth status accepted the aforementioned conditions and decided to work toward a culmination of Commonwealth status which would leave Puerto Rico a near-sovereign country -- eliminating all traces of colonialism -- and perhaps end the seemingly interminable fights between the proponents of Commonwealth, Independence and Statehood.

In the 1960s the Popular Democratic Party asked the U.S. Government to join it in naming a U.S.-Puerto Rican Status Commission (STACOM) to study the three alternatives to the status problem and present them to the Puerto Rican people for decision in a plebiscite.

The leaders of the Popular Party thought that the free vote of the people in the plebiscite would determine Puerto Rico's destiny once and for all: that if Commonwealth status won, a committee would be formed to work toward its culmination, and Statehood and Independence supporters could abandon their causes.

Commonwealth status did in fact emerge as the preference of the people in the 1967 plebiscite, but the question of Puerto Rico's political status didn't go away. In the very next year Puerto Rico elected a pro-Statehood government for the first time.

But in the 1972 elections the Popular Democratic Party regained power. Another committee (the Ad Hoc Advisory Committee) was then named jointly by the U.S. Government and the administration of Puerto Rico, with the task of seeking greater self-government and autonomy for the Commonwealth.

But even though the work of the Ad Hoc Advisory Committee proceeded slowly, and its American members proved reluctant to grant the

Commonwealth any rights that individual American States did not have, the Committee's final report recommended a greater degree of self-government for Puerto Rico than it now has. Although inplementation of the Committee's report would not eliminate all the reservations many Puerto Ricans have concerning the island's current political status, nor would it remove all the sting from charges that Puerto Rico is little more than a U.S. colony, it would in the eyes of its defenders represent a first step toward the culmination of the ideal of the Free Associated State. To be implemented the report must be approved by the U.S. Congress. Popular Democratic leaders hope the report will pass with flying colors -- but should Congress reject Puerto Rico's proposals, it would face the unhappy task of justifying its rejection before world public opinion.

The primary problem of the Ad Hoc Committee's report is that it does not lead toward a final decision on Puerto Rico's political status. And if Commonwealth status cannot be made permanent in a fashion acceptable to both parties then it must die -- if not in ten years then in twenty, and if not twenty then in thirty. And in the meantime, the status debate will continue to absorb a disproportionate amount of the time and energy of the leaders of the island's political parties.

On the other hand, the great majority of the people of Puerto Rico are understandably more concerned with the current economic and social problems that directly affect their daily lives: the high cost of living, unemployment, overpopulation, crime.

During the first decade under Commonwealth status Puerto Rico maintained an extraordinary rate of economic growth. The Economic Development Administration (EDA) promoted or assisted in the establishment of more than 500 enterprises, many of them branch factories of large Continental firms engaged in light industry. The chief inducements for businesses to locate in Puerto Rico were ten to twelve year moratoriums on insular taxes and lower wage rates for local labor than prevailed in the U.S. Net profits were substantial -- 30 percent or more was not unusual -- but the fact that most of this income left the island disturbed many Puerto Ricans. Factories, luxury hotels and other establishments were built for prospective occupants as government investments.

The EDA was not solely responsible for economic growth during this period. Early in the forties several plants (glass, cement, paperboard) were built and owned by the government, but were later sold to private enterprises. All utilities, except the telephone system, were still publicly owned. (Today all utilities, including the telephone system, are owned by the government.) Publicly authorized gambling, chiefly horse racing, casinos and a government lottery, provided additional revenues. And industries and banks controlled primarily by Puerto Rican businessmen also grew. In fact, the economy changed its predominantly agricultural basis so rapidly that by 1956-7 net income from manufacturing exceeded that from farming by 40 percent. Wages also rose during this period -- by 18.5 percent, or more than three times faster than in the United States. Meanwhile the cost of living rose at the same pace as on the continent.

But by the second decade of Commonwealth status things began to change. Many of the factories attracted to the island by the moratoriums on local taxes left as soon as the ten-to twelve-year grace periods expired, suddenly leaving many Puerto Ricans without jobs. Today, with the effects of recession, the economy remains sluggish, unemployment continues to rise, and ever greater numbers of people have given up trying to find work.

Even in the mid-fifties, a time of relative prosperity, unemployment had remained serious: in 1957 13 percent of the total labor force, 84,000 people, could not find work. But by March of 1974 the Commonwealth Labor Department's Bureau of Labor Statistics officially reported 148,000 persons unemployed on the island, and in August of 1975 the official unemployment figure stood at 19.8 percent, with unofficial estimates ranging from 25 percent to 30 percent. In June, 1975, the Commonwealth's Personnel Office said there were about 60 people applying for every available government job. And over 250,000 families and individuals had incomes below the poverty level of $2,000 per year.

Two primary factors influence the employment and income situation in Puerto Rico today.

The first is the accelerated population growth on the island. Overpopulation is, indeed, often considered Puerto Rico's foremost problem. In 1974 the island's population stood at over 2.9 million, with a density of over 800 per square mile -- one of the highest in the world.

The second is a frightening inflation that affects each and every person living on the island. Prices have been rising at a dizzying rate, and wages and salaries seem to buy less with each passing week.

In addition, although the economic situation looks grim, as it does in most parts of the world today, Puerto Rico's political leaders must devote significant portions of their energies to resolving the question of the island's political status, so that they can turn all their efforts toward solving its urgent social problems as soon as possible.

Whether the Puerto Rican people choose independence, U.S. statehood, or the development of a more autonomous Free Associated State, they must be aware the Puerto Rico should not fear being small. Greece and Israel are small countries, yet the Greeks gave culture to the West and the Jews gave religion. Puerto Rico doesn't pretend to be something it is not, for Puerto Rico knows its mission: to forward the message of its spirit -- its people's love for creation, their esthetic appreciation, their rationality, their humble religious piety, and their capacity for living together in peace with others.

CUBA

David Mitchell

Cuba, like the Dominican Republic and Puerto Rico, was largely neglected by the Spanish government until ten years after the end of the great European wars in 1815, when Spain had lost her wealthy Latin-American colonies on the mainland. But from 1825 on, the Spanish government increased its interest in and control over its Caribbean possessions, which provided migration outlets for Spaniards in times of increasing economic difficulty at home.

The settlers and administrations arriving in this period, however, aroused the hostility of the local residents whose families had been there for centuries. A series of sporadic and indeterminate conflicts between the early settlers and the Spanish government began around the middle of the century, and culminated in the bloody Liberation Wars of 1868, 1875 and 1895. By their end Spain had crowded into Cuba alone an army larger than the entire force she had maintained in Central and South America during the Wars of Independence there.

Spain never trained the Cuban-born elite to hold public office. They were eventually decimated by her oppressive armies and impoverished by the disintegration of the sugar industry.[1] (The number of sugar mills on the island fell from 2,000 in 1850 to 207 in 1894.) And when U.S. forces conquered the island in 1898, 200,000 of its inhabitants fled back to Spain, leaving almost no local leadership to maintain a republic capable of resisting external aggression or domination.

The United States took advantage of this situation to escalate its investments in Cuba, which by 1913 had risen from $50 million to $220 million, and by 1929 had climbed to over $1.5 billion -- one quarter of all U.S. investments in the Latin American sub-continent.

---

(1) Robin Blackburn, "Cuba and the Super-Powers" in *Patterns of Foreign Influence in the Caribbean,* (London: Oxford University Press, 1972), pp. 122 ff.

The nature of these investments, as Robin Blackburn observes, was as important as their size in throttling the island's elite and integrating its economy into the American system. Half of Cuba's cultivatable land was given over to sugar cane, and half of the sugar area was controlled by U.S. corporations. The investable profits from the sugar industry went to U.S. shareholders instead of remaining to develop the country. The lands of traditional Cuban owners were expropriated, or the owners were reduced to *colonos*, dependent on the credit and purchasing policies of the U.S. corporations. Cuban frustration and bitterness toward American imperialism, toward Cuba's "colonial" status as part of the U.S. economic empire, can be understood when we reflect that between 1925 and 1956 Cuba's population doubled, but annual sugar production had declined by half a million tons.

The corruption of all Cuban governments after America's intervention, and U.S. control of and assistance to those regimes which became repressive dictatorships -- Machado in his second term and Batista -- set the stage for revolt. Such examples as "the huge personal pay-off received by Batista from ITT in 1957 in return for a rise in the telephone rates" were commonplace, and the extent of collusion between the U.S. Government and U.S. financial interests in Cuba may be gauged by the fact that the United Fruit Company, with its large Cuban sugar interests, retained the Dulles family law firm as its legal advisors even during the time John Foster Dulles was Secretary of State.[2]

Gangsterism, domestic and imported, also did its share. "The character of the Cuban army was significantly changed by Batista's Sergeant's corp which replaced the old officer class... The Batista regime had a strong gangster element within it from the outset."[3] The notorious Meyer Lansky, a companion of Batista's, owned the second largest hotel in Havana, and the Kefauver investigations revealed that Havana was a major staging area for American Mafia operations. It is hardly surprising, then, that the tourism developed by American capital in the Havana area was not of museums, cathedrals or even beaches, but of brothels and casinos. . . nor should it be surprising that when American media swamped the island, proclaiming through television and educational material the values of public morality, efficiency and formal democracy, Cubans saw the U.S. as blatantly hypocritical, saying one thing but

---

(2) Hugh Thomas, *Cuba: The Pursuit of Freedom*, (London, 1970), pp. 686-687.

(3) Blackburn, *ibid.*, p. 127.

brutally inflicting quite the opposite on Cuba through the Americans who came in to control the country's economy.

When the Batista regime finally crumbled under the weight of its own dictatorial corruption and before the onslaught of the Cuban revolutionary forces of Fidel Castro, the U.S. Government naturally sought control over "the new movement." Representatives of the U.S. military mission, which had stuck with Batista's forces to the very end, offered Castro their services. He replied, however, that as he had just defeated the army they advised, he evidently did not require their assistance.

It has been suggested that the Cuban Revolution turned toward Soviet Russia because of the crude power politics of the Eisenhower and Kennedy administrations: the reduction of the sugar quota, the economic blockade, U.S.-directed attempts at invasion, sabotage and assassination, the refusal of Western oil companies to process cheaper oil from Eastern European countries in their Cuban refineries. It is also alleged that the Revolution could only have succeeded with Soviet economic help.

But on the third anniversary of the Revolution in January, 1962, the U.S.S.R. did not mention "socialism" in its greetings to Cuba. Not until the May 1st celebrations of that year did the U.S.S.R. acknowledge that Cuba had "embarked on the path of building socialism." And while Castro was publicly aligning Cuban international positions with those of the Soviet Union, he was isolating and defeating internal pro-Soviet factions,[4] at a time when Russia's Latin American strategies called for attacks on the economic structures of U.S.-supported dictatorships, as opposed to the support of armed revolts which Cuba favored. Anibal Escalants, the leader of the Cuban Communist Party, was once denounced as a "sectarian," and on a second occasion was imprisoned for trying to gain internal control over the Revolution and link it with the Soviet Communist Party in Latin America.[5]

The most famous U.S. attempt at regaining control of Cuba was the Bay of Pigs invasion of April, 1961. The C.I.A. had arranged for Cuban refugees in Florida to be trained on a large coffee estate in Guatemala, guarded by Guatemalan troops. It had spent $1.2 million improving an airstrip near the estate for the Florida-Guatemala airlift, staged by

---

(4) Blackburn, *op cit.*, pp. 134, 135.

(5) Blackburn, *ibid*, pp. 131 ff.

the B-26s of the air force it has sponsored. Its fliers had a practice bombardment when they suppressed a Guatemalan army revolt at Puerto Barrios.[6]

Despite newly-elected President Kennedy's misgivings and the fact that the veil of secrecy surrounding the Bay of Pigs invasion was pierced by Professor Ronald Hilton of Stanford University, the exercise was mounted. The landing force was taken by trucks and by air to Puerto Cabezas, on the Caribbean shore of Nicaragua. The air force attacked Cuban airfields on April 15th, but a concluding strike on April 17 was aborted. Castro's air force was saved to decimate the invasion fleet, and the 1,400 invaders of the Bay of Pigs surrendered to 20,000 loyal Cuban Revolutionary Forces.[7]

In 1962 the Cuban Government had reason to fear that another invasion was being planned with the assistance of U.S. military forces: U.S. marines were actually planning autumn exercises in which they were to overthrow a tyrant named "Ortsac" (!) on a Caribbean island.[8] By September the Cuban government had concluded an agreement with the U.S.S.R. to establish missile bases. But when the "Cuban Missile Crisis" came, Cuba resented Khruschev's unilateral actions in excluding Cuba from the negotiations with the U.S. and refused to sign the Test-Ban Treaty of 1963. Relations between Cuba and the Soviet Union cooled.

Since then Cuba has been struggling to restructure its economy and social and political institutions. The U.S. blockade has isolated Revolutionary Cuba from the rest of the Western world, which is therefore deprived of much factual information about the country. In 1971, however, the Caribbean Churches' Ecumenical Consultation for Development, held at Chaguaramas, Trindad, demanded piercing of the veil.[9] The following years saw Caribbean countries, including independent English-speaking ones, establish diplomatic and trade relations with Cuba, and in 1976 the Caribbean Conference of Churches sent a delegation there. A member of that team gives us his impressions of Cuba in Part Four of this book, followed by brief quotes from a few leading Cuban theologians.

---

(6) Sir Harold Mitchell, *op cit.*, p. 12.

(7) Sir Harold Mitchell, *ibid.*, pp. 11 ff.

(8) Thomas, *op cit.*, p. 1387 n.

(9) CADEC (Christian Action for Development in the Caribbean), *Called To Be*, (Barbados: CADEC, 1973), pp. 6, 8.

THE CARIBBEAN AND CANADA

David Mitchell

Canada's Atlantic provinces were settled at the same time as some of the English-speaking Caribbean countries, and over the centuries Canada has assumed increasing importance in the lives of Caribbean peoples.

Canada served as a transit point for slaves of loyalists resettling in the Caribbean during the British armed struggles against the U.S.; also for Caribbean rebels, like the Maroons of Jamaica, on their roads to exile in Sierra Leone or elsewhere.

When trade blossomed between the Caribbean and the North American colonies -- closer than Britain, and with wide varieties of raw materials -- Canadian commerce met West Indian needs for regular supplies of food, which spoiled quickly in the tropics, and timber, which warped if stockpiled for too long. Colonial ships, which were smaller and less expensive than British ships and could make more trips per year, carried produce to the Caribbean, West Indian sugar to Britain, and British manufactures back to their home bases.

Most of the Caribbean trade was, of course, with the American colonies. By 1772 one-third of the 672 ships carrying West Indian produce to Britain were American-built. By the period of the American Revolution, the Canadian provinces claimed only 1/11 of the Caribbean trade in salted fish.

After American independence in 1783, however, the Canadian colonies were given the opportunity to replace the U.S. as the Caribbean's major supplier. But because loyalists fleeing from the U.S. to Ontario had first claim on surpluses from the Maritime provinces, Canada could not supply everything the Caribbean needed. Some U.S. goods were allowed into the Caribbean, but the trade had to be carried in British-owned ships. These developments led to the expansion of ship-building, lumbering and fishing in the Maritimes.

Beginning in 1793 the Napoleonic Wars forced British ships to withdraw from the West Indian trade, leaving a vacuum which sparked a trade war between the U.S. and Nova Scotia. In 1820, Nova Scotia exported 30 percent more to the West Indies than she imported. The trade war ended in 1830 when British signed trade agreements with the U.S. despite the protests of Canadian interests, but Canada continued to benefit increasingly from trade with the Caribbean. In 1828 Nova Scotia exported 33 percent more to the West Indies than she imported, and in 1875, 476 percent more. An 1881 trade agreement between Canada, the West Indies and Brazil led to regular and frequent mail service by steamship between these countries, provided by Canadian interests.

Toward the end of the century the opening of the American West drew all U.S. surpluses of salted fish with it, and put an end to American salted fish exports to the West Indies. And in 1898 U.S. conquests of the Philippines and Puerto Rico, along with special arrangements with Cuba, swept British West Indian sugar from U.S. markets.

Canada signed preferential trade agreements with the British West Indies in 1912,[1] and further agreements in 1926 led to the establishment of strong trade links through the famous "Lady Boats" of the Canadian National Steamship Line (although the line remained a subsidized operation).

From the end of the nineteenth century to the present, Canada has for the Caribbean increasingly assumed the stature of a medium-sized imperial power.

By the end of the century Canadian insurance companies had penetrated the Caribbean market, and by 1966 they had more than $325 million worth of insurance in force there. Canadian banks also entered to mobilize local savings—as one observer puts it, to draw West Indian savings from beneath West Indian mattresses. They have infused no Canadian funds into Caribbean countries, but have traded on the West Indian capital they have collected, and have exported their profits back to Canada.[2]

---

(1) C. Bruce Fergusson, "The West Indies and the Atlantic Provinces: Background of the Present Relationship." *The West Indies and the Atlantic Provinces of Canada*, (Halifax: Institute of Public Affairs, Dalhousie University, Halifax), No. 52, 1966, pp. 23-32.

(2) Daniel J. Baum, *The Banks of Canada in the Commonwealth Caribbean*, (New York: Praeger Publishers, 1974), pp. 16, 26.

The Colonial Legacy

The problem Caribbean governments face with banks and insurance companies is that the investments they make with deposits and premiums from their Caribbean customers are made on behalf of the institutions, not of their clients. Whether this money is invested in manufacturing, trade, tourism, etc., in the metropoles or in the Caribbean, clients find their money used to allow banks and insurance companies to increase their control over entire economies. And profits go to the institutions, not to the people whose money they have mobilized. Caribbean people thus see their money used to finance investments outside the Caribbean, or to give banks and insurance companies more control over Caribbean economies for private and not national profit.

Canadian investment has expanded to Caribbean public utilities, manufacturing, and mining, especially of bauxite (aluminum ore). The prospect of increasing Canadian control in the Caribbean led Professor Duncan Fraser of Acadia to warn, in 1966, against Canadian interests investing "in such a way as will involve a transfer of scarce and precious West Indian resources into foreign hands."[3] It would seem obvious that Canadians who are becoming increasingly apprehensive of growing U.S. control over their resources cannot afford to become similar predators in dealing with the weaker Caribbean. But the example of bauxite will show that "Canadian interests" do not agree.

By 1966 the British Caribbean supplied 90 percent of North America's bauxite needs. But of every dollar's worth of finished aluminum produced from Caribbean bauxite, mining companies in the Caribbean (themselves subsidiaries of giant North American aluminum companies) earned only 18 cents. The remainder "accrues in the U.S. and Canada to the smelting end of the operation." And of this 18 cents, only half became income for the Caribbean. The other half, representing the mining subsidiaries' profits, went to North America.[4]

Revenues and expenditures of mining companies in the Caribbean are subject to serious manipulation by North American "parent" companies, which direct their "field offices" to produce specific quantities of bauxite for sale at cost or low profit to refining or smelting divisions in the U.S. and Canada. If the same bauxite were sold on the open

---

(3) Duncan Fraser, "The W. I. and Canada: The Present Relationship," *The West Indies and the Atlantic Provinces of Canada*, p. 38.

(4) Kari Levitt, "Strategies for Economic and Social Development in Underdeveloped Areas," *ibid.*, p. 6.

market it would bring far higher prices, on which Caribbean governments would get increased taxes. Furthermore, payment is not necessarily made in foreign currency, but may be credited against charges for goods and services supplied to the mining companies by metropolitan subsidiaries of the parent companies. And Canadian and U.S. firms have steadily resisted pleas from West Indian governments to transfer more of their smelting operations to the Caribbean. Amid stiffening Caribbean opposition to these "predatory" types of investments, Guyana, Surinam and Jamaica have nationalized their bauxite industries. An example of what can happen when a country moves to make the most out of its assets is supplied by Guybau, a government corporation set up by Guyana to run the DEMBA (Demerara Bauxite Company, a subsidiary of the Aluminum Company of Canada) plant it took over in 1971. Its production and profits exceed those made at any time while the company was owned by Canadian investors: sales leapt from $39 million in 1973 to $214 million in 1974, while profits after tax rose from $8 million to $19.1 million.[5]

When we turn to the subject of Canadian aid to the West Indies, we find "good intentions tempered by confusion." The aid comes with strings attached: whether it is in the form of outright grants or loans with high or low interest repayments, at least 80 percent of it must be used to buy Canadian goods and services. Even if Caribbean or other goods and local expertise were available and eminently more suitable for projects undertaken with the aid funds, they could not be bought. Nor at first would Canada allow governments receiving loans to "sell" the amounts of the loans to commercial interests so they could import other, more salable and useful Canadian goods, and use the proceeds of the sale to buy local goods and services more suitable for the projects being aided.

Beginning in 1958 Canada donated $10 million over a five year period to the now defunct West Indies Federation. More than half was spent building two passenger-freight vessels which were never free from technical breakdowns and brought the infant Federation annual deficits of $500,000—instead of the small profits it had made through the use of chartered vessels which had inaugurated its shipping service some years before. A University hostel in Trinidad, schools, airport facilities,

---

(5) "Caribbean Monthly Bulletin," Puerto Rico: Institute of Caribbean Studies, University of Puerto Rico, Vol. 9, Numbers 5, 6, May-June 1975, p. 13.

warehouses, surveys, teachers and specialists were all provided. In 1966 the Caribbean received $10 million in aid as contrasted with $430 million received by Southeast Asian countries under the Colombo Plan.[6]

Critics of Canadian aid point out that the strings attached (use of Canadian materials, experts and plans) leave West Indian materials, experts and plans idle. And West Indian governments taking Canadian loans are, in effect, borrowing against their future earnings to pay for the privilege of supporting Canadian skills and manufacture. If Canada had to receive aid from the U.S., would Canada willingly have the U.S. impose such restraints? In fact, were these restraints imposed on European countries when the U.S. gave them aid for postwar reconstruction under the Marshall Plan?

Canada has been receiving West Indian immigrants. The fact that many have been East Indians is a tribute to the influence of missionary work by the United Church of Canada and the Presbyterian Church of Canada in Trinidad and Guyana. Canadian universities have also had great influence in offering higher education to Caribbean people over many decades. Fraser warns, however, about restrictions placed on colored West Indians as contrasted with treatment given to Italians, Germans and Eastern Europeans. West Indians, he says, are mostly "to be assigned to the more menial tasks in our society. This is comment enough about Canada's immigration policy!"[7]

Caribbean people have had satisfying personal contacts with Canadians over the last few decades. Educational opportunities and missionary concern by Canadian churches have generated good will. But the policies of the Canadian Federal Government and Canadian trading and investment institutions on aid, assistance, immigration, trade and tourism have made Caribbean peoples increasingly suspicious of the apparent growth of Canada as a medium-sized imperial power, primarily interested in Canadian profits from Caribbean investments in banking, insurance and manufacturing. And why, we ask, were Canadian troops sent to Jamaica some years ago to join the Jamaican forces of the former right-wing J.L.P. Government in jungle-warfare training? There are no jungles in Canada. Developments such as these, and closer examinations of current Canadian policies toward the Caribbean, are beginning to wipe

---

(6) Duncan Fraser, *loc. cit.*

(7) Duncan Fraser, *op cit.*, p. 40.

out the historical and present assets of our relationships with Canada, and are making us turn our eyes toward other peoples less concerned with their own welfare, more willing to consider their responsibilities as neighbors to weaker peoples and cultures.

part 2

a look at the caribbean economy

A LOOK AT THE CARIBBEAN ECONOMY

David Mitchell

(based on a paper by Carol Keller)

The political divisions of the Caribbean and the political fates of Caribbean countries have been determined by the way the region has been developed by the business and trading interests of its colonial or neo-colonial masters and exploiters, the metropoles of Britain, France, Holland, Portugal, Spain, and in recent times, North America.

European settlements in North America evolved quite differently from those in the Caribbean. The proprietors of the thirteen American colonies rapidly found their settlers acting in their own needs and interests and demanding self-government. The War of Independence those colonies launched in 1776 was essentially the eruption of basic conflicts of interest between the settlers and their British proprietors, among whom were the Kings of Britain. And even in Canada, the trading interests of the huge Hudson Bay Company failed to control and exploit the colonists of the Maritimes, the Great Lakes and the Prairies.

In the Caribbean, however, the development of the sugar cane industry, beginning in the 1650s, gave rise to plantation economies. Here the large plantations, with their powerful European financial backing and access to cheap imported labor, (slaves and later indentured workers,) swallowed up the small farms of the first settlers. A history of Barbados, one of the Lesser Antilles, notes that by 1682, 12,000 European settlers had emigrated -- "wormed out of their small settlements by their more subtle and greedy neighbors" -- leaving only 700. Many went to the American colonies, most often to the Carolinas (and in fact, seven of the first 23 governors of South Carolina came from Barbados.) At the same time, the number of African slaves in Barbados rose from 6,000 to 46,000. In short, in the growth of the Caribbean economies, but not in the growth of the North American ones, "the movement of people followed the movement of capital and enterprise."

A Look at the Caribbean Economy

Caribbean countries have been kept underdeveloped -- or rather, developed for backwardness -- by the very ways in which they have been built, as colonies, into the economic and political structures of their respective metropoles. Colonial or neo-colonial subordination has dictated that local people will remain in the lower-paying jobs; that minerals, lumber and agricultural produce will be exploited too rapidly, leading to the exhaustion of natural resources and the denuding of lands; that profits from all stages of industries depending on raw materials from the Caribbean will be spent to develop the metropoles, and even to block the development of local competing industry within the Caribbean.

Within these exploited Caribbean countries, people on the margins of the metropolitan North Atlantic economy "have been incorporated in a way prejudicial to their interests: the poor get poorer and the rich richer."

The Caribbean countries (except for Cuba, which is a special case) now face a common host of difficult, sometimes critical, economic problems.

The Caribbean countries were small to begin with, and endowed with limited -- although sometimes very rich -- resources. Their populations are increasing rapidly, leading to labor surpluses which can no longer be relieved by wholesale emigration. Except for those with petroleum or bauxite resources, they depend almost totally on a narrow range of export crops -- bananas, citrus, cocoa, coffee, pineapples, spices and timber.

But whatever their products, Caribbean economies face above all a continuing rape of their resources, in which their raw materials are exported to metropolitan markets and not used according to any planned pattern of production or consumption within the region or for the benefit of its people.

The first of the three cases studied in this section examines the problems faced by Caribbean agriculture, where the colonial "plantation legacy" has carried through in the monopolization of land and the control of production for the benefit of giant metropolitan-based corporations. As we have seen elsewhere (for example, "The Church and the Socio-Economic Situation in Guadeloupe,") mechanization of plantations has also led to widespread unemployment: the people who should own or control Caribbean land are increasingly denied even the opportunity to earn "plantation wages" working it for foreign interests.

A similar situation obtains with tourism, the subject of the second case study below. Here we are warned of the emergence of the "tourist plantation" economy which, under foreign ownership or control, reduces Caribbean people to positions of servitude in their own countries.

And finally, an analysis of who controls and profits from the exploitation of Caribbean bauxite resources reveals once more an all-too-familiar pattern -- although here some Caribbean countries are beginning to combat their problems through nationalization of their bauxite industries, increased taxation or both.

The development of manufacturing in the Caribbean, which along with that of tourism has largely taken place since World War II, also deserves a brief mention here.

Industrial production has not had the desired results. As many jobs have been lost through declines in traditional agriculture and self-help, labor-intensive industries as have been gained through the establishment of new industries, and local value added to manufactures have been small because most raw materials and machinery must be *imported* at high costs. Industrial development has been systematicaly unsuited to countries with growing labor forces, and the situation has been aggravated by increases in the costs of imported manufacturing components, which then increases the costs of manufactures and the balance-of-payments deficits of local economies. And in the end, large percentages of the profits from Caribbean manufacturing are remitted overseas to the foreign owners of the enterprises.

Attempts to finance local industries with foreign capital, so the Caribbean will not have to import so many manufactured goods, have brought conflict between the new manufacturers and the traditional commercial importers. The result has not been replacement of imports through the manufacturing of local raw materials. Instead we find new industries in the Caribbean importing components and raw materials to be "assembled" locally, and *these* replace imported finished products. Local economies are further damaged when these spurious "local industries" gain protection of their markets through prohibitions on the import of similar finished products from outside the Caribbean, and end up as monopolies. And as with any foreign investments, financing of these new industries in the Caribbean has led to a drain abroad of capital from their profits in the forms of interest and dividends to shareholders -- or profits are plowed back to extend mortgages on and control of the raw materials of the region.

A Look at the Caribbean Economy

In recent decades manufacturing and tourism have modified the Caribbean economies created by early trading and capital enterprise. Now, in the late twentieth century, multi-national corporations are increasing their controls over Caribbean economies, swallowing up all local development and stifling local initiatives. Through all these developments the structures for perpetuating foreign exploitation have remained intact. The continuing operation of these structures amounts to nothing less than a continuing rape of the Caribbean's resources, and therefore of its people, by the metropolitan powers.

PLANTATION AGRICULTURE IN THE CARIBBEAN

based on a paper by Carol Keller

The links between the economies of the Caribbean countries and those of the major metropolitan nations determine the agricultural policies and actions of Caribbean governments, their options for agricultural development, and the operation of such factors as the extent of small farmers' participation in investment possibilities. These links, in turn, can only be understood through an analysis of the plantation system and its impact on the Caribbean.

A plantation or estate is an economic unit which provides agricultural produce for export. In the Caribbean this produce is primarily from tree-crops rather than from livestock, except in a very few cases like Cuba, the Dominican Republic, and Guyana. Major crops have been sugar, cocoa, coffee, citrus, bananas and spices.

A plantation is composed of a minority of skilled supervisors and administrators and a large majority of unskilled workers. It is run as part of a larger economic unit based overseas in the metropole which includes processing and marketing. The same foreign owners may have plantations in many different Caribbean countries producing raw materials for their metropolitan processing and marketing operations.

The large majorities of unskilled labor imported to follow the flow of European capital and enterprise into the Caribbean consisted of slaves from West Africa and indentured workers from countries outside Europe. Political control of Caribbean countries, unlike that of America or Canada, remained overseas and international, and under it they experienced mercantilism (against which the U.S.A. rose in revolt), slavery, free trade, capitalism, imperialism, and more recently, mere political independence. These historical forces have determined the principles and laws by which their plantation systems operate. The financial and industrial centers of the systems are at the sources of their capital, where the owners use their political influence to control prices for plantation products, tariff structures, prices for plantation imports, loan funds for the whole enterprise, and ultimately the ways in which the resources of the producing countries are used.

Production patterns of large plantations, in turn, affect the ability of surrounding peasant farmers to produce and make profits. Peasants are not another sector of the society, but are evidence of how the plantation sector has penetrated the entire system. Despite differences in types of export crops (coffee, cocoa, sugar, bananas, etc.) or in the location of the financial seat of control of plantations (U.S.A., Britain, France, Holland) the effects are universal. The Caribbean is a cultural sphere with the characteristics of monoculture, multi-racial societies, and weak community cohesion (not to be confused with the co-existence and accomodation of established minority groups—dualism or pluralism). Also typical are small peasant proprietors with similar crops, production techniques, marketing arrangements, cuisine, folklore, music, tradition, and values which determine the tone of social life.

The largest tracts of land owned by foreign companies are alienated from occupation by local peasant farmers. When the land is exhausted it is left idle and new land is opened up -- a wasteful process which is good for giant corporations like the United Fruit Company, Unilever, Tate and Lyle Ltd., the Booker Group of Companies, etc., but which countries with limited amounts of arable land can ill afford.

Giant corporations control agricultural production according to their own objectives, diverting Caribbean land from domestic production needed to feed growing populations and to offset the blossoming taste patterns for foreign imports occasioned by income rises and by lowered domestic production. These giants dominate the agriculture of their host countries, and in many cases their economies as well. Their self-sufficient operations, which extend from raw-material production to the marketing of processed products, including shipping, bring them returns which are often greater than the host country's revenue from its total agricultural output.

The plantation economy has an inherent tenacity, strengthened by the fact that no one corporation depends on the output or economy of any one plantation country. Metropolitan corporations will operate wherever their colonial products earn foreign exchange and there are adequate supplies of material for export, along with roads, transport, ports, power, and other infrastructure requirements. These firms can allocate resources adequately between their plantations overseas and their processing and distributing subsidiaries at home, but they fail to allocate efficiently *within individual units* -- the plantations (viz., systematic land waste), the refineries, etc.

At times metropolitan peoples themselves have been manipulated into subsidizing these industries. In one instance the British Sugar Board bought Caribbean sugar from British firms and sold it at a *lower* world market price to the refinery subsidiaries of these same companies. In turn the refinery subsidiaries sold it at a *higher* price than that at which they had bought it from their parent companies through the subsidy funds provided by the Sugar Board. Here inefficiency of operation is concealed by subsidizing.

In addition to diverting Caribbean land from meeting local food needs, plantation economies, through tariff preferences granted to their agricultural products, generally restrain land and capital from moving into better combinations with available labor to create additional employment and income. In determining its real profit from the presence of sugar plantations, for example, a Caribbean country must deduct from its sugar revenues: 1) revenues repatriated to foreign investors, 2) extra costs of buying manufactures as the result of reciprocal trade agreements, and 3) the dynamic cost involved in not putting the land to better use in the local economy, such as raising cattle for meat and dairy products.

An illustration of the restraints placed by the plantation system on diversification of agriculture in the Caribbean lies in the fact that the total food import bill for the Commonwealth Caribbean in 1973 was $225 million, and in 1974 it rose to $500 million -- but inadequate protein and calorie supply still demanded $75 million worth of supplementary imports.

The conclusions of an examination of the plantation system in the Caribbean are inescapable: the system stultifies agricultural development and perpetuates a purely outward-looking strategy which serves only to encourage maintenance of the structures that mis-allocate Caribbean resources and further the development of under-development.

TOURISM IN THE CARIBBEAN

Neville Linton

Tourism has been an established industry in the West Indies since the beginning of the century, but it first became of major significance to most of the islands in the postwar period. Given the proximity and affluence of North America, it is not surprising that the great majority of visitors are from the U.S., with Canadians second. North Americans tend to come in the winter months, although in recent years some Afro-Americans have come in the summers. U.S. visitors constitute 80% of all tourists to the Bahamas, Bermuda, Puerto Rico, the U.S. Virgin Islands, and Jamaica; Canadians, Europeans and other West Indians make up a significant proportion of tourists to the islands further south.

Tourism is the largest item in world trade, and is attractive to underdeveloped economies as a major source of foreign money. In some countries, such as Spain, Hong Kong, Panama, Mexico and the Bahamas, it is the mainstay of foreign exchange. But only in a few cases around the world has a significant international tourist industry been built up initially by *foreign* investments, as it has in the West Indies; and herein lie the roots of the Caribbean tourist industry's problems.

A healthy tourist industry in today's world must be characterized by a high proportion—indeed, a majority—of local ownership, or tourism will merely acerbate international relations, not only in terms of the developing political attitudes in the exploited countries, but because of reactions abroad. Riots in Curacao can lead to pickets in Holland or Jamaica or New York. The era of the plantation economy must end in the Caribbean and the era of the "tourist plantation" must not be allowed to develop.

Whether or not there is a majority of local ownership -- which may be difficult to achieve in very small societies such as that of the Bahamas -- the management of tourist industries must be predominantly local. This is a natural corollary of nationalism and of mutual respect of peoples. It will not do for people to be but servants, highly paid or otherwise, in their own countries -- especially in a region like the Caribbean, where the majority of tourists are of different races than the local populations (as is not the case, for instance, in Spain, a major tourist country).

One cannot overlook the problem of white tourists always being waited on by black or brown servants, or of tourism appearing as one race's chance to assert its superiority complexes and aggravate the inferiority complexes of others. The descent of hundreds of thousands of rich whites upon the new tourist havens in the black world, now politically alive, is fraught with problems. Added to them is the problem of overbalanced diversion of people from agriculture and craft pursuits, and the effects on their values such diversion can have. The integrity of a sturdy peasantry is endangered by pressures which transform it into the servility of those who are always in service jobs or play secondary roles in their own society's economy.

The economic advantages of tourism to Caribbean countries must be clear and considerable, given the social costs the industry necessarily involves. By implication a tourist is someone with a financial surplus, and tourism must be seen as a mechanism for redistribution of resources around the world.

The total value added to a country's economy by international tourism is equivalent to its foreign exchange earnings from visitors' expenditures less then costs of imports needed to serve the tourist industry. So the more a country must import to sustain its tourist industry, the less valuable tourism becomes to it.

One of the most fundamental needs of the Caribbean is to localize all sectors of its tourist industry and thereby reduce the very high percentages of imported goods used by tourists. Visitors who use local products are friends in the best sense, as their stays have benefited the society. The reputation of Americans as tourists who require services, food, etc., to be "just like back home," is not one that furthers brotherhood.

In addition, the Caribbean is particularly wary of the increasing desires of the rich or well-off in temperate countries to invest in second houses in the tropics. Such absentee ownership, or landlordism when the properties are rented, will be as intolerable as foreign-owned hotels if it reaches a significant scale. It holds no meaningful economic benefits for the small host countries, who find the properties becoming pawns of speculation in American real estate markets, which then absorb the profits from Caribbean real-estate transactions. The fear is that if imperialists cannot take Third World countries by conquest, they will try to buy them up.

Concern with the negative aspects of tourism has been mounting in the Caribbean, and in recent years it has been accompanied by demands that the industry be reshaped to benefit the region.

In 1971 the Caribbean Conference of Churches' development agency CADEC hosted a consultation on tourism which led the governments of the region and the tourist industry to set up the Caribbean Tourist Research Center, and CADEC went on to contribute to its support. Thus a drive has been mounted to establish small, owner-managed hotels and guest houses which appeal to tourists whose incomes are not as high as those catered to by the region's traditional luxury hotels. The practice of setting up enclaves of foreign culture and privilege for tourists is now disappearing, and in most places it is no longer legal to establish private beaches for tourists only. Planning is replacing random development of tourist facilities. Attempts are being made to protect environments and replace imported food with local produce.

But in addition to these largely affirmative steps, there have been increasing calls for defensive measures against alienation of land and tourist-sparked inflation of both land and commodity prices beyond local standards.

Measures to defend against alienation of culture are also necessary. Cultural forms are sometimes modified to make them more familiar to visitors, and they are generally vulnerable to the dynamism of the American impact—as seen in many Caribbean people's desires to use the American accent, dress like Americans, and acquire American goods. The aggressive influence of American culture is personified in the arrogant style of some U.S. tourists.

A healthy tourist industry holds mutual cultural benefits for hosts and guests, and a tourist should be able to learn enough about Caribbean countries and their peoples to respect them. When North Americans travel to Europe, even to the sunny Mediterranean, they do not go just for the sun, the surf and the entertainment, but also to absorb cultures they have been schooled to respect. Especially in a contemporary world in which the issues of development and fair distribution of resources are emerging as the major challenge of our century, tourists in the Third World ought to use their visits for education as well as pleasure. They can no longer exclude themselves from the problems of their fellow men. The privilege of travel now carries with it the imperative of sensibility.

Sensibility is needed in cultural affairs as well as economic. Caribbean peoples, for instance, do not appreciate their image as "sexy" when it implies whites coming south to taste "exotic" sex. The result is prostitution, male and female. In the West Indies it has been largely male, as female North Americans have apparently come looking for "kicks," or reaching for fruits that are forbidden in the discrimination of their own environments. Sexual relationships should be based on respect, not cash purchasing "novelty."

Tourism in the Third World is only valid as an industry if its social and economic benefits to host countries clearly outweigh its costs. In the past, when Caribbean governments were either colonial or impotent, such calculations were academic. But Caribbean peoples are increasingly resolving that this will cease to be the case in the future. Furthermore, Caribbean tourism will only be meaningful if it develops as an industry which caters as much to domestic tourists as to foreigners.

Today's tourist to the Caribbean has the opportunity to assess the effects of the region's history first-hand, and to examine the system of exploitation of the underdeveloped by the developed. He also has the responsibility not to confuse poverty with the exotic.

The Caribbean is a beautiful environment. Its cultures are a fascinating New World melange, and its people are friendly. Its welcome to tourists will only continue, however, if tourism serves to create a more humane Caribbean society.

THE CARIBBEAN BAUXITE INDUSTRY

Anthony Gonzales

Bauxite is a mineral ore from which aluminum, a basic metal, is derived. Like oil, it is one of those primary raw materials whose acquisition on cheap terms from Third World countries has long been vital to the industrial development of the North Atlantic nations- although oil, for instance, is today far more widely recognized as such. But one has only to begin to list the innumerable industrial uses of aluminum in the manufacture of everything from consumer durables, machinery and electrical products to cars, aircraft and missiles, to recognize the significance of cheap bauxite for those nations which consume it. And one has only to begin to examine the relationships between those nations and the bauxite-producing countries to find increasing wealth and prosperity in the former and cumulative underdevelopment and poverty in the latter.

The Caribbean's bauxite-producing countries -- Guyana, Jamaica, Surinam, Haiti and the Dominican Republic -- are the center of the industrial world's backward bauxite hinterland. For more than half a century they have been part of an international aluminum corporate system which, in the interests of its long-term growth, has organized a flow of Caribbean bauxite to feed its various plants in North America and Europe.

Alcan established its operations in Guyana as early as 1917, and five years later North American companies started mining bauxite in Surinam. These firms have subsequently taken most of their bauxite from these countries, and have gained control over bauxite resources there to ensure reliable supplies in a world dominated by the imperatives of survival. Compared with the 1930's, when most bauxite in the Western world came from North Atlantic sources, Third World countries now contain a practical monopoly of bauxite resources, and at present 40% of the world's production comes from the Caribbean, with Jamaica and

Guyana accounting for 20 percent and 10 percent respectively.[1]

The great bulk of the bauxite mined in the Caribbean is exported to smelting plants in the U.S., Canada and Western Europe, but a small proportion is processed locally into alumina (aluminum oxide, later transformed into aluminum), and at present one-quarter of U.S. alumina imports come from the Caribbean.[2]

The giant North Atlantic aluminum corporations, backed by their governments, gained long-term concessions for the exploitation of bauxite from Caribbean countries on favorable terms during the colonial era, when Caribbean governments had no influence in such matters, or at times of nominal sovereignty, as in the cases of Haiti and the Dominican Republic. It is in this context that we must attempt to assess the dominance of these metropolitan companies, the ways in which they have reduced the effectiveness of Caribbean states in promoting their own economic development, and the extent to which they have contributed to the underdevelopment of the entire Caribbean region.

In terms of control, a few American-based multinational combines, such as Alcan, Alcoa, Reynolds and Kaiser, manipulated the Caribbean bauxite situation (except in Guyana, which nationalized its bauxite industry in 1970). Decisions on vital aspects of an industry which accounts for 70 percent of the exports and the bulk of state revenues of these countries are made by these four companies, and are geared to maximizing the companies' long-term profits instead of developing Caribbean domestic economies.[3]

One of the major consequences of the Caribbean governments' lack of control over such decisions is the negligible value added to bauxite in the countries where it is mined. Value is added where the bauxite is processed, and as Norman Girvan notes, "When we export 7 million tons of bauxite it is worth L18 million; the alumina content of this bauxite is, however, worth L75 million, the aluminum content L272 million, and as 'semi-finished metal products' it is worth L650 million."[4] It is obvious that the transfer of the last two stages of aluminum production to the Caribbean would be of crucial importance to the develop-

---

(1) *U.N. Statistical Yearbook*, 1970.

(2) U.S. Department of Interior.

(3) Huggings, H.D., *Aluminum in Changing Communities*, I.S.E.R., 1965.

(4) Girvan, N., et. al., "Unemployment in Jamaica," *Readings in the Political Economy of the Caribbean*, p. 272.

ment of Caribbean economies. But alumina processing did not begin in the region until the late 1950s and early '60s, when newly independent countries began to demand that the companies advance the stages of local aluminum processing. And even though local economies can produce and deliver alumina more cheaply than the companies' metropolitan operations, processing has remained concentrated in North America because of the special needs of the four multi-national corporations and their metropolitan-oriented perspectives. An aluminum smelter has been constructed in Surinam, but it is owned by Alcoa and is used to penetrate the European market.

Another area in which the metropolitan companies enjoy a large measure of control is price-fixing. Due to their "vertical structures," they are involved in both buying and selling, and can manipulate prices in order to maximize their profits. Depending on how they set prices between their subsidiaries, their profits can appear in their bauxite mining operations, in their alumina or aluminum processing phases, or in their shipping operations.[5] As a result of such manipulations the price of Guyanese bauxite remained the same from 1938 to 1959 while the price of that mined in the U.S. doubled -- even though Guyanese bauxite is of a higher grade.[6] The effect of price-fixing has been to keep revenues to the bauxite-producing nations relatively low. A recent export levy imposed by Jamaica illustrates how underpricing has historically affected revenues: in one year Jamaica's new tax is expected to increase its bauxite revenues sixfold.

Growing realization by Caribbean nations that ownership and control of their bauxite resources have traditionally been alienated from the objectives of their own development has ushered in a new era, which coincides with the world-wide search by Third World countries for a new economic order based on more remunerative prices for their dwindling mineral assets. Guyana's nationalization of Demba–Demerara Bauxite Company, a subsidiary of Alcan (Canada) and Reynolds (Guyand) Mines Ltd., a subsidiary of Reynolds Metal (U.S.) was precipitated by the fact that after forty years, because of the Guyanese Government's lack of effective decision-making power, alumina processing was still only a small part of the local operations of these companies. The success of Jamaica's export levy has prompted similar actions

---

(5) Girvan, N., "Why We Need to Nationalize Bauxite and How," p. 219.

(6) Reno, Philip, "Aluminum Profits and Caribbean People," *Imperialism and Underdevelopment*, R. Rhodes, ed., New York, Monthly Review, 1970.

or plans for them by Guyana, the Dominican Republic, and Haiti. Meanwhile the Jamaican Government intends to increase its ownership of Jamaican bauxite and alumina operations.

Perhaps most promising, Caribbean countries have taken the initiative in the formation of the International Bauxite Association (IBA), whose goals, like those of O.P.E.C., are to ensure better prices for their products and increase national controls over their industries.[7] If IBA's members act in a cooperative fashion, it will be able to dominate the world bauxite market. Further, the Caribbean countries whose resources are so vital to North American markets are strategically placed to take certain steps against the huge North American aluminum companies. The fact that these countries can export significant portions of their recent increases in taxes on bauxite to North American consumers reflects, in part, the advantages of their locations.[8]

These new strategies, based on the aspirations of the Caribbean people to own and control their natural resources, should go a long way toward redressing the historical imbalance in the relationship between the underdeveloped bauxite-producing countries of the Caribbean and the developed bauxite-consuming nations of North America and Europe.

---

(7) At present the IBA consists of Jamaica, Australia, Guyana, Surinam, Guinea, Sierra Leone and Yugoslavia. The Dominican Republic has announced its intention to join. These nations control 80% of world bauxite production.

(8) Gillis, M., and Charles McKive Jr., "The Incidence of World Taxes on Natural Resources with Special Reference to Bauxite." *American Economic Review*, May, 1975, pp. 389-396.

part 3

the changing face of the caribbean

THE CHANGING FACE OF THE CARIBBEAN

If this book's first two sections have successfully demonstrated that Caribbean peoples are becoming increasingly aware of the common sources of their problems, they should also suggest that analyses of the region's needs are underway, which in turn give rise to positive suggestions for meeting them. As the following two excerpts from *The Changing Face of the Caribbean** indicate, its author, Irene Hawkins, is a firm proponent of regional unity; of seeking regional solutions to regional problems.

The first excerpt concentrates on the Caribbean's needs to overcome the tensions that have arisen in its societies as the result of its historical legacy. In this connection we might recall P.I. Gomes's observation that in Guyana it was the deliberate policy of the British Colonial Office to maintain separation between ethnic groups for the purposes of controlling them. The second excerpt deals with Caribbean education, which desperately needs to be brought out of its archaic orientation and made relevant to the region's contemporary needs.

---
*Published in Barbados by Cedar Press, 1976. Includes end maps. $7.95 (U.S. price) plus postage.

SOCIETY AND ITS TENSIONS

Irene Hawkins

The multi-racial and multi-cultural facets of Caribbean society may be fascinating for a visitor, but this fragmentation has created tremendous social, political, and economic problems both within many Caribbean societies and among the different territories. This 'balkanization' and lack of homogeneity is holding back both the unifying process within many of the territories and the area's political and economic integration as a whole.

The degree to which both racial and cultural influences have been absorbed in the past in a particular country has differed substantially from territory to territory, with far-reaching consequences for the present structure of society and its feelings of national identity.

The optimists will say that gradually all the different races and cultures will be absorbed in the Caribbean melting pot and that a more or less cohesive society will emerge one day, but judging by developments in the past this seems too simple a view. Of course there has been a lot of mixing and intermarriage. It is also true that most politicians and Prime Ministers are black; but a 'white bias,' perhaps strongest in the French territories as the ones most strongly tied to metropolitan origins, still very much permeates the thinking and the attitudes of the older generation in the Caribbean who grew up during the colonial days. Even in a supposedly well-integrated society such as the Puerto Rican one, it seems still valid to say that the lighter-skinned a person is the better are his chances of being socially acceptable and economically successful. It seems a far cry from racial integration when in Puerto Rico it is still very much harder for a black person to reach the top position than for a white. In fact, the number of really successful black businessmen and academics in Puerto Rico is astonishingly small. Occasionally the government may appoint a black person to a leading job for appearance's sake. This does not alter the fact that there seems little contact between the majority of white and coloured Puerto Ricans on the one hand and the black minority on the other. Because of the limited leverage of the black population, this may not constitute a 'black power' dynamic, but it certainly does not make for a stable society.

Many observers maintain that the stratification of Barbadian society according to the subtle degrees of skin colour is one of the most rigid in the area. It certainly seems that the economically dominant white Barbadian—that is, the planters and the leading traders of Bridgetown —stick very much to themselves both socially and business-wise. It was virtually impossible, until fairly recently, to break into this "charmed" circle. It is only a few years ago that coloured businessmen came to the fore and that the doors of the Barbados Yacht Club were opened to selected black visitors. The very close and uninterrupted links with Britain since the early colonial days, the continuing strong economic position of white people and, because of that, the much stronger emulation of every nuance of British life up to the present day, have all contributed to make Barbados into a "little England," which it was rather sarcastically called by its Caribbean neighbors.

In other Caribbean territories the descendants of Dutch or French settlers and more recent European immigrants still call the tune and thus, in effect, tend to prevent unconsciously the emergence of any local way of life and culture.

Guyana, Trinidad, and Surinam contain another source of potentially serious racial conflict—the coexistence of a large Negro population alongside an often equally large and faster-growing East Indian sector, who tend to have larger families than Negroes. Some people feel that in the shorter run the mounting tensions between these two groups are even more serious and explosive than the white-versus-black economic conflict.

All three countries boast about their multi-racial harmonious societies, but it is questionable whether the fundamental cultural and economic differences between the two main races can ever be bridged. Traditionally, the Negro has tended to be educated for the civil service or professions in the town. The Negro enjoys life and spends money while the East Indian, who succeeded the Negro as identured labourers on the sugar plantations after the slave emancipation during the last century, tends to lead a family-bound and thrifty life so as to give his numerous children a decent education. Frequently, one meets a poor-looking Indian farmer or worker who will point out property he owns and talk about his children studying in Canada or the United States. Now the possibly explosive point has been reached where an increasing number of young, educated Indians are challenging the traditional Negro dominance in the professions of law and medicine and in the civil service.

So far only Guyana has gone through the ordeal of mutual massacre, between 1962 and 1964 [and this, it has been alleged, was instigated from outside Guyana's border. See "Guyana," by P.I. Gomes. Ed.] The Guyanese Negroes, although by now in a minority (they account for only about 30 percent of the total population against the East Indians' more than 50 percent, the rest being mainly indigenous Indians, known as Amerindians, and Europeans) are clinging to power under their Prime Minister, L.F.S. Burnham. Some people argue that the landslide victory of Mr. Burnham's People's National Congress in 1973 could not have been possible without a good deal of Indian support. So perhaps the Guyanese are at least departing from their traditionally racial voting pattern and some sense of national unity is emerging. That is at least how the optimists would like to interpret it. But more likely the pessimists who fear a quasi-dictatorship and open conflict sooner or later will be proved right.

In Trinidad the much more rapidly increasing East Indians have by now probably outstripped the Negro population, but Eric Williams' governing Negro party has so far benefited from the lack of discipline among the Indian opposition. In Surinam, too, the East Indians (or Hindustanis, as they are called there) have recently become a more numerous ethnic group than the Negroes, accounting for about 37 percent of the population. While there was a Hindustani/Negro coalition government the danger of a political polarization along racial lines seemed averted. In fact, the Hindustani majority party then was far-sighted enough to offer its much smaller Negro coalition partner an equal number of ministerial posts in the government. But the fact that the present government does not represent the Indian voters must inevitably lead to a growing sense of frustration among that section of the population and in the Hindustani opposition party. The horror of a repetition of the Guyanese massacre may help to keep emotions down and, in addition, the multi-racial membership of the emerging trade union movement should in time be an important counterweight to the racially divided political parties.

History has handed to the Caribbean very complex racial and cultural problems, to which have been added those engendered by the all-embracing influence of North America, whether in the field of entertainment and leisure, type of housing, dressing, or eating. This influence makes progress toward any local racial or cultural unity virtually impossible. The many imports from the United States, the constant flow of tourists into the area and of Caribbean visitors up north, the many expatriates working in the area and, above all, the continuous bombarding of the Caribbean people with American radio and television programmes inducing them to live and eat and think "American," all prevent the radical shift in Caribbean attitudes and values which has to come about if the "new Caribbean Man" is to emerge.

Of course, long-term metropolitan domination is responsible for this disorientation. Until recently most Caribbean people just allowed themselves to be swamped, but in the last few years there has been a definite trend towards local ownership and direction of television and radio stations, newspapers and other mass-media. With a young post-colonial generation growing up, young politicians taking over, the increasing demands for more local economic control, the search for a national and, ultimately, a Caribbean identity and culture is intensifying. At the moment it is mainly confined to the young Negro girls and boys and some of the older intellectuals in the English-speaking territories who are supporting Afro hair-styles and African dress, and are trying to spread the message that "Black is beautiful." In some neighbouring countries the adoption of the Guyanese shirtjack (a lightweight fusion of a shirt and a jacket) instead of the stifling dark suit in government and business offices is a case of point. "Doing your own thing" has become a much used phrase in Trinidad and Tobago.

Governments are fostering this new trend with local and regional art festivals where dances and songs of African origin are being revived. There are exchange visits of theatre groups, but very often they are desperately short of money. Guyana is setting up its own College of Arts. The first pan-Caribbean Art Festival—CARIFESTA, held in Guyana in August 1972—revealed the immense fertility of the Caribbean in dance, song, painting, and poetry. The second CARIFESTA was held in Jamaica in July 1976.

It is often falsely maintained that there is no indigenous culture and art in the Caribbean. It is true that much of the cultural heritage was lost long ago and that local talents are not as rich and varied as in a society which has developed homogeneously. But in fact the lack of local interest and of a large enough market for local literature and arts of all sorts, rather than of talent and originality, are the main obstacles. West Indian books are much easier to obtain in either New York or London than in the leading bookshop in Barbados. Some of the territories, for example, Jamaica, Guyana, Haiti, and the Dominican Republic, have lively local communities of artists, playwrights, poets, painters, dancers, and musicians. Guyana, Trinidad, and Jamaica have very good local theatre groups, often performing plays written by local people. Jamaica's National Dance Theatre Company under university lecturer Rex Nettleford has done a great deal to revive old dances and is highly regarded both in and outside the Caribbean. Trinidad and Tobago's newly founded National Dance Company had a successful debut in London in the summer of 1972.

After the Second World War Trinidad and Tobago was also the cradle of the steel-band, now popular far beyond the Caribbean. One can discover some superb modern paintings and drawings in the little art galleries of old San Juan or Santo Domingo, and every visitor to Haiti longs for one of those enchanting primitive paintings, crowded with exotic animals and flowers a la Henri Rousseau. The Episcopal Cathedral in Port-au-Prince is adorned with unique Haitian interpretations of religious themes, the precursors of a developing movement in indigenous religious art.

But as yet most Caribbean people do not believe in their own values and talents. History has left the Caribbean in a state of psychological and mental subordination. For centuries all the cultural and intellectual impulses, new ideas and values, have come to the Caribbean from Europe and, more latterly, from North America. Many people feel that they are not able to create anything new themselves, and suffer from deep-seated inferiority complexes. Perhaps this is the most serious and most difficult source of tension within Caribbean society today. A growing number of people argue rightly that unless Caribbean people can liberate themselves from this mental colonial bondage and gain confidence in themselves and in their abilities to shape their own way of life, the cutting of their political and economic ties with their former masters will give them only a superficial and unsatisfactory kind of freedom. As one of the foremost thinkers in the Caribbean, William Demas, described it so aptly in a graduation address at the University of the West Indies:

> Decolonization in the West Indies, as in other parts of the Third World, is a process of renewal, of building anew, of striking out on one's own—a process by which a liberated people creates new structures, new institutions and, above all, new attitudes and new values. Decolonization is a total integral process, one of attempting to create a New Man and New Society, one of innovating—or at least intelligently adapting from other countries—in every conceivable field of human endeavour. A decolonized society is a creative society; and a creative society is a self-confident one. Decolonization therefore begins in the mind.[1]

This does not mean that the Caribbean should or indeed would want to cut itself off from cultural and intellectual influences from abroad altogether (and it would be suicide to become economically insolated); but instead of the one-way flow of ideas as in the past, there has to be a two-way traffic. There is no doubt that the Caribbean has a lot to give to its own people and to the outside world. Furthermore, the present wealth of Caribbean culture could be greatly enhanced if the many Caribbean artists living in North America and Europe, where financial returns and public response are much more rewarding, could be tempted to return home and if, above all, teachers in the area started right from the earliest stage of education to awaken an interest in all aspects of local and Caribbean life, rather than trying to produce a model Frenchman, Englishman, Dutchman, or North American.

Education plays a crucial role in instilling that sense of pride and self-confidence which in turn will be the key to creating a feeling of Caribbean unity and identity, free from the shadow of the past.

---

(1) William G. Demas, "The Prospects for Decolonization in the West Indies," *Change and Renewal in the Caribbean*, (Barbados: The CEDAR Press, 1975), p. 53.

EDUCATION AND ITS IMBALANCES

Irene Hawkins

It would be wrong to belittle the advances the colonial administrators achieved in the education field in the area. The coverage of the school system at both primary and secondary level goes much further than in many other less-developed countries and, as we have indicated above,[1] literacy rates are high by international standards.

The area spends a large part of its budget on education and a good deal of aid flows into this sector which, as everybody agrees, is vital to future development. Nevertheless, the present educational facilities —both on an elementary and on a higher level—are far from adequate both in quantity and quality. Above all, present-day Caribbean education is not geared sufficiently to the area's particular economic and social needs. In fact, the contents of the curricula and the skills and values they instill in the pupils are not only outdated and unsuitable, but in many cases are positively harmful to the area's economic and social development and the emergence of a Caribbean identity.

The common mistake that has been perpetuated in practically all the territories, whether they were under French, Dutch, British, or in recent years American tutelage, has been to try to train clerks versed in the famous three "Rs" (reading, writing and arithmetic) and administrators able to quote Shakespeare or Racine—imitators of a metropolitan style of life. What is needed rather are down-to-earth people with an understanding of and interest in agriculture, small-scale business, and the local culture, with the will to make their lives within the local urban and rural community.

---

[1] Irene Hawkins (*The Changing Face of the Caribbean*, p. 28) indicates that literacy rates have risen significantly: in Puerto Rico from 68% to 88% in thirty years, in English-speaking islands up to 90%. Cuba has eradicated illiteracy. In Haiti only up to 10 percent of the adult population is literate.

In secondary education, for example, languages rather than relevant subjects such as Caribbean history and geography still feature prominently. The aversion to science and technology continues right throughout to university education and, as William Demas critically observes, "Even where the content is right, the orientation is wrong. The teaching of science and mathematics is not oriented to locally relevant areas such as accounting, business management and agriculture; nor is civics oriented towards subjects as co-operatives."[2]

In his opinion, in probably all Commonwealth Caribbean countries the whole secondary school system is counter-productive in terms of objectives like the creation of employment and orientation of young people towards agriculture and rural development. School and work are completely divorced and the emphasis is on formal rather than out-of-school training.[3]

[*Hawkins goes on to point to other areas where the worlds of school and of work are successfully integrated, such as Denmark, Cuba, and China, and to say that educational co-operatives should be developed in the Caribbean to produce graduates capable of replacing foreign managers and technicians. Ed.*]

But perhaps even more important than producing appropriate skills, schools and universities have a vital role to play in instilling a sense of purpose, the desire to achieve something in life.

In the past centuries there was no point in the ordinary black slave striving particularly hard in order to climb the ladder: class, colour, and family connections decided who rose in society, how far and how fast. This sense of pointlessness of any effort must inevitably also influence people's attitudes towards work. When outsiders dismiss high unemployment with the simple explanation that people "just do not want to work," they show how little they understand the complex psychological problems that lie under the surface of a happy-go-lucky attitude towards life. Very likely this missing urge to be successful in life is also at the root of the all too apparent lack of business entrepreneurship and efficiency. Society has put no premium on being go-ahead and

---

(2) William G. Demas, "Is the present approach to economic development planning relevant to the solution of the human resource problems of the Caribbean" (mimeo), paper given at Human Resources Seminar, UWI, Mona, Jamaica, August 1970, p. 6.

(3) William G. Demas, "Youth and Development," *Change and Renewal in the Caribbean*, (Barbados: The CEDAR Press, 1975), p. 24.

innovative, so why bother? Obviously a society's set of values and norms cannot be swapped overnight for a new set, but any change towards a new Caribbean person will have to come largely through schools and universities.

This in turn will require a fundamental re-orientation of the majority of the teachers who, by and large, are just not willing nor equipped to venture into new avenues, away from the traditional set of subjects and ways of presenting them. Foreign technical assistance in education has not exactly encouraged teachers to be Caribbean-oriented. Too often in the past, technical assistance programmes have sent teachers and technical experts into the area who knew nothing or too little about its values, problems, and needs. Teachers' training facilities need to be upgraded and expanded and the teachers motivated differently, so that more and better-trained teachers, capable of instilling a new, locally-oriented meaning into education, emerge from them. As the Tripartite Survey on the small English-speaking islands pointed out in 1966: "Up to 50% of the instructors in most elementary schools are untrained and possess only an elementary schooling themselves. These people tend to copy methods by which they were taught and hence their low calibre of instruction is a self-perpetuating condition of elementary education."[4]

The other important means of affecting a re-orientation of the Caribbean people must be to educate as many people as possible from primary right through university graduate level inside the Caribbean. The Caribbean territories must have their own universities, technical colleges, and specialist institutions such as hotel schools. Otherwise research and teaching which is suitable to their particular economic and social problems will just not develop sufficiently. The University of the West Indies, with three campuses in Jamaica, Barbados, and Trinidad, was established as late as 1948; since then it has become the foremost source of new ideas in the English-speaking Caribbean. But apart from the Dominican Republic, Guyana, Haiti, Puerto Rico, and Cuba, the rest of the Caribbean countries are not so fortunate as to have their own universities.

There is still no institution of higher learning in the French-speaking Caribbean, and the French government, intent on preserving the departments' adulation of everything French, is obviously not likely to

---

(4) *Report of the Tripartite Economic Survey of the Eastern Caribbean*, (London: Her Majesty's Stationery Office, 1967), p. 4.

finance such a local move towards cultural and intellectual independence. In Surinam efforts at building up a fully-fledged local university were basically confined to establishing the two faculties of law and medicine and adding, in the early seventies, some technical degree courses. There was no faculty of economics or social science to spawn a good many of the 'radical' intellectuals, as in the English-speaking countries.

Ultimately it is, of course, the willingness to identify with one's native country and culture that matters, as the number of eminent foreign-trained U.W.I. lecturers who have spearheaded the change in Caribbean thinking shows. Generally speaking there is no doubt that because so many Caribbean students still have to go to foreign schools, universities, and specialist colleges, there exists a very great risk of psychological alienation from their home environment among the very people who may hold influential positions in government and business on their return from abroad. Probably many will not return in any case because the foreign way of life and the greater scope for bettering themselves both financially and socially will be too much of a temptation. So to a considerable extent the brain-drain has its roots in the defects of the Caribbean education system, and the sooner these are removed through improvements in education the better.

[*Hawkins comments that the countries of the Caribbean need to extend the joint use of their technical and university resources to train more people within the Caribbean, even if they must be exposed afterward to study abroad. Ed.*]

If the signs of growing separatist thinking within U.W.I. circles is anything to go by, the hopes for a strong regional university seem very bleak. It would be fatal, both psychologically and economically, if the various campuses were to confine themselves to serving a particular part of the Caribbean and thus discourage the free flow of students and dissemination of ideas throughout the area. But the action currently being undertaken to re-study the role, function, and organization of universities in the Commonwealth Caribbean offsets this pessimism in the eyes of some observers.

part 4

voices in culture and religion

VOICES IN CULTURE AND RELIGION

The following statements, more personal in nature than what has come before and dealing with culture and religion, convey something of the current mood of Caribbean Christians in facing the challenges and promises of their common future.

"A Summary Report of a 1976 Visit to Cuba" is extracted and edited from an account by one of a team of observers from the Caribbean Conference of Churches which visited Cuba at the end of January, 1976. It is followed by brief quotations from contemporary Cuban church leaders.

STRUGGLING TO BE

William W. Watty

Pelau is a favorite Trinidadian lunch on Saturdays, but the recipe is simplicity itself. You put all the leftovers from the past week -- rice, peas, bits of chicken and pork, ox tail and salami, whatever you can scrape together from the refrigerator -- into a pot, lace the concoction with pepper and seasoning, stir well, and cook. This meal of leftovers is usually the most delicious meal of the week.

Caribbean peoples are like a Pelau. As long as they see themselves as *diaspora*[1] from other lands, separated and estranged from each other, they are no more than the leftovers of humanity, and to speak of Caribbean culture is a sick joke. Imitate Europeans and we are caricatures of Europeans. However Indian we are, India is what is really authentic. Try as we like to be African, Africa is better.

But look at a West Indian cricket team of African, Indian and European descent, and you see the Pelau coming out in a style which is not imitative of the English, but far superior. Look at a Caribbean woman walk or smile or dress or dance and you see a style and grace which cannot be duplicated anywhere else in the world. Look at a Caribbean mother bringing up her brood singlehanded, against overwhelming odds, and you find a fortitude and a skill which is well-nigh superhuman. Listen in on West Indian wit and humor, especially when West Indians poke fun at themselves, and you might begin to understand why we have survived in circumstances under which any other people might long since have succumbed. Pelau is the art of making do ... in style.

The more overt manifestations of Caribbean culture -- the Steel Band, the Calypso, the Reggae, the Carnival, and even the "grass-roots" religions -- are the windowdressing of something very deep and genuine which pervades the Caribbean's whole social consciousness. Here survival

---

(1) *Diaspora*, a Greek word meaning people of a particular culture who have become displaced persons and exiles dispersed throughout several countries.

depends on making do with what one has. And while one is at it, one might as well do it in style. Lively imagination and free improvisation have produced not only the Calypso but the rum, not only the Pocomania and the Jordanites but the common-law unions, not only a University spread over three campuses but a cricket-pitch on a cul-de-sac. New languages have emerged: the Creole of Haiti, the Labrish of Jamaica, the Papiamento of Curacao, the Patois of St. Lucia and Dominica. And the Caribbean has produced an impressive array of world-renowned authors such as Roger Mais, Vidia Naipaul, Samuel Selvon, Aimee Cesaire, C.L.R. James, and George Lamming.

But the *Pelau* society has not yet produced its own theologian, in spite of the facts that Caribbean societies are saturated with religion and that Caribbean churchmen have won academic distinctions for themselves in the institutions of Europe and America. The reason is simple: Caribbean churches are committed to foreign theologies. These are imported by missionaries or imbibed by Caribbean people abroad, while missionaries, for reasons best known to themselves, are dedicated to frustrating the emergence of a Caribbean theology.

The one area where a Pelau culture has no place is among the churches, where creativity and imagination, experimentation and improvisation, are anathema. In this respect, at least, all the foreign-based churches, from the Roman Catholic to the Seventh Day Adventist, are bedfellows. Whether theology in the Caribbean emanates from Europe or North America, it must remain foreign. Graham is divine, and Montini is master of "them that know."[2] The irony is that while changes are taking place at the sources of imported theologies, in the Caribbean tributaries Catholics remain Tridentine, Anglicans Tractarian, Methodists Wesleyan, Lutherans Martinist, Baptists Ana-baptist, and the Reformed Church remains Calvinist.[3] We somehow feel obliged to perpetuate theological quarrels whose instigators declared amnesties long ago. And so every September we have come to expect the descent of the "evangelists,"

---

(2) This refers to the unquestioned acceptance in some conservative religious quarters of Billy Graham's statements and also the Roman Catholic doctrine of Papal infallibility. (Pope Paul was formerly Cardinal Montini)

(3) The writer uses each term to indicate that some Caribbean denominational adherents still accept the views held by the parent European denominations two to five hundred years ago. For instance, "Martinist" is used as a reference to the adherent of some Lutherans to Martin Luther's position on theological and other issues.

who will tell us once again what they have told us a hundred times before, and what we can now tell them far better (and with better accents) -- "The Bible says this" and "The Bible says that," and "May the Lord bless you *real good*!"

And so the religious and cultural oppression of Caribbean peoples and the imprisonment of their spirit continues under North Atlantic hegemony, as Caribbean culture continues to be frustrated by *everything* American, from Madison Avenue and Wall Street to Hollywood to the Yankee dollar itself.

Nowadays those of us who have no consuming desire to visit the United States find it more and more difficult to travel within the Caribbean without stopping over in Miami (if you please!) and sampling the book-stalls in its airport. And C.I.A. agents in the Caribbean must certainly be the most leisured class in the world: they have nothing to do but gloat.

The crowds that cue up at the U.S. Embassy in Kingston and endure all kinds of humiliation and dehumanization in hopes of getting to the "Paradise" north of the Rio Grande must give immense satisfaction to somebody (whatever our local politicians say).

But for myself, I say, "To hell with it!" I believe the Caribbean has something better struggling to be born. Up to now we have only seen glimpses of it, or sensed its stirrings in the womb -- but it is there. And those of us who, thank God, have been bitten by the bug will not be enticed, however much we are tempted. Dump your leftovers where you will, if you can afford to. I will relish my Pelau to my dying day.

THE MANY FACES OF JAMAICA

Alfred C. Reid

Is Jamaica a land of freedom where the natural rhythms of the human spirit encounter no unreasonable impediments, or is it a prison from which Jamaicans must escape in order to preserve their humanity? Is it a land of multi-racial harmony, or is it in fact one of history's most tragic examples of racial oppression? Is our swinging calypso/reggae, rum-guzzling, smiling "tourist image" a mere commercial contrivance, a hideous hypocrisy, an heroic attempt to present our best face to the world while we secretly nurse our pain? Or is it a true picture of the triumph of the human spirit in the face of terrible odds? Are we, in fact, a creative, resourceful and hard-working people who have made something beautiful out of nothing? Or are we a slothful, undisciplined, selfish people, imitating the consumer cultures of some of our wealthier neighbors while neglecting to develop our own great human and natural resources?

There is a rich and a poor Jamaica, a white and a black, a rural and an urban. There is a third world Jamaica and a metropolitan Jamaica, and the two exist independently, sometimes practically oblivious to each other. But the violent social confrontations of recent political actions suggest that these two Jamaicas are becoming aware of one another. At the same time, it is possible to say that the concept of two Jamaicas is inadequate to describe our present situation -- not because the two have merged into one, but because we now have many more than two Jamaicas: capitalist Jamaica, Rastafarian Jamaica, agricultural Jamaica, the Jamaica of the urban middle class, of unionized labor, and even Christian Jamaica, each struggling to capture territorial Jamaica for itself and defeat, suppress and control the others. Jamaica is up for grabs, and the struggle has attracted some interesting newcomers. The Nation of Islam (a Black Muslim group), at the opening of a new temple on Charles Street in Kingston, recently announced their intention to make Jamaica a Muslim country in ten years.

The religious scene in Jamaica reflects the contradictory nature of the society. Jamaicans are said to be a deeply religious people, and there is evidence for this in the institutional and social power of churches and other religious groups. Nevertheless, religion has always operated at the circumference of Jamaican life, like a highly prized ornament one would not wish to part with, but which is safely locked away most of the time.

Christianity has enjoyed a virtual monopoly in Jamaica over the past three hundred years. The most significant alternatives have been Pocomania (Pukumania) and other revivalist cults, and Rastafarianism, a more recent but very powerful black nationalist messianic movement. Both of these movements, however, are to some extent reinterpretations of Christianity, and therefore indirectly witness to its monopolistic position.

Christian churches, in the meantime, flattered by political patronage, social prestige and international support, have tended toward complacency. Their bitter struggles -- especially those of the Baptist and Methodists -- against the slave masters, their pioneering work in education, social welfare and community development, their successful efforts to keep hope and humanity alive in the darkest hours of Jamaican history, are all matters of record. Furthermore, since they were alone in attacking these problems, their mistakes as well as their achievements are to their credit, since only by doing nothing could they have avoided the mistakes they made. Nevertheless, the Christian community must accept in all humility that its cautious and conservative positions have helped in the long run further to entrench exploitation, oppression and misdevelopment.

The problem now facing the churches is that Jamaica is not simply underdeveloped; it is misdeveloped, and in a way that requires the poor to accept their suffering so a few may enjoy abundance. So necessary is the poverty of the poor to the existing social order that any serious attempt to redistribute wealth is regarded, perhaps with some justification, as an attempt to destroy the society.

Because of their relatively unchallenged positions, the churches in Jamaica have never had to do much theology of their own. They are quite accomplished at grasping other people's theologies, but interpreting Jamaican realities in the light of the gospel is quite another matter. So some of the most venerable but theologically naive churches in the world now find themselves confronted with new situations not at all envisioned by the liturgies and theologies they have borrowed from abroad. Jamaicans of the type who used to be ignored -- the poor, the disinherited, the marginal citizens -- are identifying with the Third World, the poor world, the black and colored world, in their search for common solutions to common problems. Automatic alliances with white Western Christian democracies have not, after two hundred years, produced the kind of solutions Jamaican problems call for.

Christian and other conservative elements in the country sometimes speak of the "unfortunate phase" (violence and political murders) through which Jamaica is now said to be passing. Some people will not or cannot accept that we are at this time witnessing changes of a nature and scope that make them irreversible, even if they are subject to false starts and temporary setbacks. One of the major political parties has adopted as its slogan, "Turn them back." But the present movement to social action and change, aimed at the transformation of society from its roots up, is more broadly based than previous ones, and is capable of attracting more international support from groups and nations interested in Third World development. Under the circumstances, it seems strange that there is an absence of theological reflection on the situation.

Because of the past and present roles of the Christian churches, many of those at the forefront of the struggle do not identify with them. Christians ought not to see this as a threat, nor should churches permit themselves to be used by alienated minorities as refuges from change or pressure-groups to resist it. The churches must grasp with courage and faith the great new opportunities for service open to them at this time. They need theologies of mission which will reaffirm their commitments to the people of Jamaica rather than to oppressive value systems and foreign cultural patterns, and they need to make clear that they are fully capable of carrying out their missions not only in the context of a capitalist system, but under whatever system will most truly benefit the majority of Jamaica's people.

By the sincerity of their purposes and the usefulness of their ideas, the Christian churches should put themselves in positions to contribute to the present ideological debate. To do this they will have to be more theologically serious, more socially responsive and responsible. Social responsibility will involve taking sides and taking risks, exposure to misunderstanding and the possibility of mistakes. But we can presume that groups which claim to be under the guidance and power of the Holy Spirit will not shrink from its responsibilities to be more Jamaican, to renounce age-old posturing and anxiousness for foreign approval, to be more innovative, and to stand with the Jamaican people in their struggle for a better life within the integrity of their own culture.

One way or another, the many faces of Jamaica will begin to reflect the unified efforts and communal life of a rich, multi-faceted culture. Christians should be at the forefront of the movement toward national unity, a unity which will bring to fulfillment the diverse talents of all Jamaica's people. Christian churches in Jamaica are now called to a special kind of ecumenicity -- not just unity with other like-minded Christians, but with people of all religious, political and social views, ideologies and aspirations, who are working for progress. The ends we have in view may not coincide and our means may differ, but our joint efforts may surprise us all with a result inconceivable at the moment from any of our limited points of view. In the meantime, in the words of one of our new reggae songs --

> While we fight one another
> For the Power and the Glory
> JAH's kingdom goes to waste.

YOUTH: THE CRESCENT GROWS AT THE MARGINS

Oscar Allen

The young are surplus people on the fringes of Caribbean society. They are vital resources, marginalized and forced to submit to the hostile interests of the few.

Marie left school at thirteen years of age. She is intelligent and pleasant. At home she continues her daily chores -- minding her mother's three babies, washing, working in the garden plot on the mountainside, and just being around. It is a full life and an empty life, the life of an extra person.

Raj left school at seventeen with five O-level certificates. In the following two years he worked twice, during the busy commercial Christmas seasons. He had wanted to do research into construction materials, but the only job he could get was packing crates in the Shandury warehouse. Raj is just another surplus person.

Kamau was a chemistry honors graduate, but his Public Service job had been mainly as a correspondence clerk. He was removed from it, primarily for mixing with the "dread" youth of Corbeau Town.[1] Now he helps in a friend's disco, spinning the wax and giving off righteous sounds.[2] He is one of society's optional accessories.

---

(1) *'Dread' youth.* This Rastafarian term has been used to describe groups who act in violent anti-social ways, with criminal overtones. It is, however, more commonly used to indicate the inevitable and severe judgement of the oppressed on the social, political, economic and religious systems that have forced them into their present deteriorating position of hunger, poverty, and hopelessness. Rastafarians use Biblical imagery, maintain a closed group, believe in a coming millennium for black people, and held Emperor Haile Selassie in divine regard. They call the traditional institutions, including institutional Christianity, "Babylon" and believe that Babylon will come to 'dread' the resistance of the under-privileged and their attempts at removal of evil conditions. They symbolize this revolt by their hairstyles or 'dread' locks.

(2) *'Spinning the wax and giving off righteous sounds'* is a language sentence using the vocabulary of Caribbean youth culture. In the language of 'society' (internationally accepted English) this would mean 'playing discs on a radiogram and amplifying through the speakers to a noise level considered acceptable by the youth present.'

Caribbean society is unbalanced by pressure against its youth from those people and interests we call "Babylon," "the ruling class," or simply "society." Young people know this class quite well. They work for it, and observe the massive profits it takes in. Young women are coerced into sexual intercourse in return for favors from its members -- even opportunities to get or keep jobs.

The ruling class accepts Babylonian Imperialism; the arrangements which limit the Caribbean's resources to profitting foreign interests. What Jesus said about binding a strong man so as to pillage his resources (Mark, 3:27) applies to our society, which has been bound and pillaged by colonial and neo-colonial penetration. The profits demanded by North Atlantic interests are not increased by the fulfillment of Caribbean youth -- the latter are left on the sidelines of history and even threatened with relative extinction through population control.

But the story of the Good Samaritan who befriended the sufferer at the side of the road is also now being applied by Caribbean youth. As the outcast Samaritan and the discarded sufferer exchanged real love and concern on the edge of the public interest, against the mainstream of public conduct, so Caribbean young people today are discovering themselves and outlining an alternative kind of life, in which they identify with and practice the lifestyle of the poor, the exploited and the discarded of all generations -- peasants, workers, the unemployed and the culturally deprived -- the bulk of our people. In this act of love between the surplus people and the suffering people, a dialogue of struggle is set up which marks an important growing point on the margins of the Caribbean Crescent.

The experiences of young people in our schools and in our society as a whole impede their creative contacts with their environments. Society tries to teach them it is irrelevant to be conscious and imaginative, wrong to be young and penetrating. Love is an option only for those who can afford the restricted convention of the one-to-one home-and-bedroom exercise. As an exercise of solidarity with oppressed people and a commitment to history, love is out of order and subversive. To be a real neighbor is to be identified as "dread."

Rather than take the risks of truly being young people, some of the Caribbean's youth submit to becoming deformed and co-opted into the disjointed system. They are induced and constrained to sell their persons for "the dish of succession." They reject fundamental dialogue with the ruling classes. But the questioning scrutiny to which Jesus submitted the apparatus of power when he visited the temple at the age of twelve was one form of the fundamental clash between the "establishment" of death and the "seedlings" of love and life.

The recent involvement of young people in deliberate and widespread movements to the land is a sign of their resistance to the policies of suffocation. It also strengthens the development of their own ideas. From Trinago (Trinidad and Tobago) in the south to Haiti in the north, the collective cultivation of land has been seen by young people as the creative basis of livelihood. Consciousness and wisdom come from reflecting on and drawing knowledge from this activities. Reactions have ranged from outright slaughter of youth, as in Dominica in 1974-5 (the present case against Desmond Trotter), to more covert insertion of these activities into tame and generalized programs.[3]

The political resistance of youth to the instruments of suffocation emerges in "labor unrest," protests against injustice on the world scale, rejection of certain types of work and study, and refusals to vote. Active cultural and political organizations and programs are a large part of the counter-policies of youth.

The idea-system young people have been developing and practicing emphasize that the person is central. The person-connected-to-nature-and-to-person is the definition of "human" among some youth. They emphasize the importance of work, of community, and of struggle against the establishment of wrong and for the establishment of righteousness. Many youth are involved in grasping the truth of idea-systems sympathetic to their own. Socialism, with its emphasis on man, class, struggle, and vision, is generally accepted as the dominant ideology of youth. It is a sometimes lyrical and melodious socialism, but it is none the less serious.

While Caribbean society is determined to underdevelop its youth, its young people are "undertaking" society. They are not a sub-culture, but are outlining the qualities of a new society and helping to destroy the sources of our present imbalance and disintegration.

---

(3) Desmond Trotter, a young dissident Dominican of middle-class origin engaged in a protest against social institutions regarded as enslaving and corrupting, was accused of the murder of a visitor during Carnival celebrations. The police investigators, who presented the evidence in the case in which he was found guilty, were later alleged by the chief witness to have bribed and intimidated her into giving false evidence. As a consequence the Government has been forced to commute the death sentence. Pressure is now mounting to strike out the whole case and to free Trotter.

At this time of intense crisis, young people throughout the Caribbean are engaged in the prophetic pursuit of life and history. As with all truly prophetic tasks, theirs is impossible to achieve unless it is connected with large efforts. Let us remember that the prodigal (younger) son, reborn in impulse, could not have regained the family circle against the wishes of his elder brother if their father had been neutral or weak. "Can the prey be taken from the mighty?" asked Isaiah. Not unless Caribbean youth and their allies discover neighbors correctly coming out to strengthen them against the dominant forces in the Caribbean and overseas. The challenge of youth calls for an imaginative and scientific rebirth of the forces of salvation on a world scale.

SUMMARY REPORT OF A 1976 VISIT TO CUBA

Jimmy Tucker

The purpose of the trip was to learn how the church has responded to the socialist revolution in Cuba, and also to learn educational strategies, agricultural and public health programs, cultural developments, etc., ongoing after seventeen years of Revolutionary government.

* * *

SANTIAGO. We arrived in Santiago, in the south, on Wednesday, January 21st. We remained until Friday the 23rd, when we left and went northwest by bus to the agricultural lands of Camaguey. We left there for Havana on Sunday, January 25th, to join the Presbyterians who were having their annual assembly. (From this experience in particular we learned to appreciate the tenor and character of liturgical worship as it reflects a vibrant and positive theological awareness.)

* * *

In Santiago we were impressed with the spotless state of the streets and the purposefulness of the people as they commuted to and from work, and there we learned vividly of the sacrificial prices that were paid by some of the heroes of the revolution.

We visited the birthplace of national hero Frank Pais, a Baptist layman, school teacher and comrade of Fidel Castro, who is remembered as the mystic poet of the Revolution. His history was particularly significant for us, as it dramatized the tendency of Baptists in many countries—as in the emancipation era in Jamaica in the 1830s—to be motivated by the Gospel to uncompromising commitments, not exclusively non-violent, to social justice. It was ironic, however, that when we met with the Executive Body of the Council in Havana to get an indepth account of the religious factor in the Revolution, we were told that "At first, immediately after the Revolution was declared successful,

Baptists hailed the slain patriot as Ambassador of Christ, but later, when the Government sought to implement its socialist policies, his name and memory became anathema." Today there is a William Carey Baptist Church in memory of a famed international missionary,[1] while the name of Frank Pais has been removed from the records of Baptist congregations in which the national hero served as an organist and choir director.

Next we visited the birthplace of Anton Maceo, who as a revolutionary is no stranger to Jamaicans. Maceo, one of the pillars of Cuban independence, holds a tremendous story for those of us who are Caribbeanists. Like Jose Marti (whose verses can be read on billboards in the streets and public places all over the country challenging Cubans to learn, work, and to respect and honour the Cuban woman) Maceo is regarded as one of the fathers of Cuban independence. He was a military strategist, poet, and political philosopher, and as such he is well known. But his writings, with specific reference to his vision of a Caribbean society that includes the free states of Jamaica, Cuba, Puerto Rico, Haiti, and others, are not widely known.

* * *

Bright children between the ages of five to fourteen years volunteer, after parental consent is given, to dedicate themselves to complete knowledge of and for the Revolution at the provincial Palace of Pioneers. Our group was absolutely impressed by the level of learning, zeal and intelligence of the young boys and girls. Their educational training is truly remarkable. They learn by practice, and the essential principle is that every object that merits intellectual attention is perceived as having a fundamental significance for Cuba. The chemical processes in the production of sugar cane, for example, were demonstrated.

* * *

On our way to the House with the Well, at the foot of the Sierra Maestra mountains (where Castro and his comrades worked out the strategy for the attack on the Moncada barracks), we met with about 350 school children, from 11 to 15 years old, who were planting seeds on about

---

(1) William Carey was a British Baptist missionary who went out to North India at the end of the eighteenth century to found Baptist missions there and develop a great literacy program.

five acres of land. From this encounter we learned of the importance given to agricultural training in the Cuban school system: agricultural training is the base of the Cuban education from the earliest grades to university level.

In Camaguey we visited an agricultural training college that is providing for the scientific cultivation of crops for new towns being constructed for thousands of workers, and learned that many students come there from Havana and Santiago. We came to the opinion that Cuba has an effective central planning capability that has resolved rural-urban dichotomies of education and the application of technology for national development. In other words, the "rural drift" to cities which creates unemployment, urban congestion, and crime in our "free societies" is nonexistent in Cuba.

* * *

Camaguey, as an agricultural area, is one of the most rapidly developing provinces in Cuba. Its recently established university offers courses in agronomy, mechanics, and physical, chemical, and electrical engineering that are relevant to cattle-raising, in addition to medicine, economics, journalism and law.

We saw thousands of apartment complexes being built for workers and their families, with many shacks adjacent to them. We were told that, at the completion of the new apartments, the shacks would be ceremonially destroyed to dramatize the improved housing conditions. We also learned that it is government policy that a worker should pay not more than 10% of his earnings for rent, and that after twelve years he becomes the owner of what he has rented.

It appears that the most interesting social developments to be found in this province are in the areas of agricultural science and engineering. The role of the Lenin Vocational Training School is quite significant. Very bright students are awarded scholarships to pursue disciplines for which they demonstrate ready aptitudes. It is an excellent model of a rural technological school that is truly reflective of a preoccupation with the comprehensive human and ecological needs of the immediate environment.

While in Camaguey we also participated in several worship services, and met a number of English-speaking people of Jamaican and other descents who talked openly about life in Cuba. At the Episcopal Church, on the Saturday evening before we left for Havana, the Rev. F. Martinez (since deceased), Vice-President of the Cuban Council of Churches, President of the Pentecostal Church, and a former lieutenant in the rebel army of Fidel Castro, delivered a stirring address, affirming that Christians ought to build socialism.

We were generally impressed with the people of Camaguey. They appeared to be loyal workers, and we were told that many, including the women, who worked on the farms belonged to the *Committees for the Defence of the Revolution*, volunteer groups of citizens -- in all numbering about 4,500,000, or approximately half the population of Cuba -- who have developed a security system that in the early years of the revolution was noted for its characteristic style of reacting out of panic. It is now a system that is being administered with maturity and confidence.

* * *

In Havana many of our burning questions on the Church's role in the Revolution were answered, and we saw how the fruits of the Revolution were being administered. We gained an appreciation of how day-care centers for the children of working mothers fit into a social system built on the principle that every human being, weak or strong, sick or healthy, sustains dignity only by "having something to do." In Havana we also understood more fully Cuba's claim of full employment. And we were exposed to one of the most dramatic examples of human reconstruction in the Caribbean; the work that is being done at the Havana Psychiatric Hospital. Our delegation observed mental patients at work in creative uses of occupational therapy based on the patients case histories and individual "in-house" observation. Scarce money is being spent on this work, which is very low on the list of priorities of "free enterprise" systems. Once again the element of cleanliness was evident, whether one inspected the ward, the chicken farm, the barber shop, the grounds, or the shoe shop. At any rate, this post-Revolutionary medical service provided a dramatic contrast with the pre-Revolutionary medical services typified in the old hospital-museum we visited in Santiago.

Among other noticeable institutions we visited was the Havana Tobacco Factory, which gave us new insights on the functions of labour unions in socialist societies and a realistic example of "worker participation." We also obtained a practical insight on just how *The People's Assembly* is going to function when it is implemented later this year on a national scale.

* * *

Our delegation was exposed to the hallmarks of the Revolution, the importance of agriculture to the development of the country, and ideas as to the reason for the way certain institutions relate in a consistent whole. I believe that there are a few areas, however, on which some more information is needed. There areas are:
1. The role of the Catholic Church prior and subsequent to the Revolution;
2. The economic scope of the system;
3. The character of the correctional institutions.

VOICES FROM THE CHURCH IN CUBA

Sergio Arce-Martinez

We must begin to open Church doors, go out into the world and relate to humans in it in the context of contemporary history of our country, and our world. We have to recognize it as it is and accept it as it is, more or less as a Marxist revolution. It cannot be any other way in the 20th century. The Christians live under the revolutionary Marxist principle of the present century, as in other countries they lived under the revolutions which occurred under the guidance, direction, orientation, and influence of other revolutionary principles....

The Church must interest itself in the affairs of man, and even though we know that "man must not live by bread alone" we know that bread is necessary to live. The Church prays "Our Father, ... give us this day our daily bread," but work is one way of realizing this prayer. There is no true prayer without commitment and consistent work. "I will rise and go to my father, and I will say: 'Father . . .' "as the Prodigal Son in the parable. When you pray, don't pray for food for yourself alone, but for food for everyone, "Give us this day our daily bread," bread we have worked for together, so we can legitimately call it *ours*.

The believer and the Church must be interested to see that society produces its materials in such quantities that each and every person receives an equal part of the bread which belongs to everybody. The Christians must have as part of this commitment the same interest which the Marxists have in the outcome, production and distribution of consumer goods. In our case, we should be specifically interested that we have a good harvest, a viable, successful economy.

We want a world which does not destroy food for economic reasons while millions are starving. As a church, and as part of our commandments, we must be interested in securing the well-being of as many people as possible, not in the abstract, but in a very concrete thing in the situations in which we live, with the resources which God has given us on this island.

Dr. Arce-Martinez quotes Huber-Conteris, Uruguayan working with ISAL (Church and Society in Latin America).

I see the Christian faith and socialism as being complementary. Socialism offers me a concrete response to the problem of social justice and helps me to understand the world in which I live, and the history of the world and the social, economic, and political processes of nations. It gives me an immediate insight into the future and offers, as an alternative, the only acceptable form of social life. But when we speak of fundamental questions, questions about destiny, the reasons for one's historical existence, the reason for the world's existence, the reason for life and living, the inevitability of death, I am forced to seek answers in another system of ideas, which are not social, neither economic, but religious: and this is the decisive question which for me judges Christian faith....

Rev. Francisco Martinez, deceased Vice-President of the Cuban Council of Churches and President of the Pentecostal Church, spoke of taking part in productive manual work:

In Matanzas, by the invitation of the National Director of the Study Center, I participated in a task of cutting cane. In Camaguey, with the coordination, I helped with the cleaning of the cane. I worked in different places of construction, directed by the study center. Participation in the work that Latin American Christian Education Commission (CELADEC) and the Student Christian Movement (MEC) have programmed. In almost all these activities there have been moments of adoration to God.

Rev. Miriam Ortega, Reformed Presbyterian Church in Cuba, speaks of the real nature of peace:

As I write these lines, I hear the laughter of the students of the Faculty for Workers, who have their study-center close by—laughter of the young adults, women, men who, with their books under their arms, walk to their center of study, and I believe that in that innocent laughter, as algebra, or economy, or history is discussed or understood, runs the indestructible thread of a peace won by the sacrifice, struggle, and effort of a people.

Of what peace could our brothers of Angola write, subjected to the brutal aggression of the imperialists, and of the oppressive forces of the racist South Africa? Of what peace could our women write: or the Chilean man brutally tortured by a fascist regime? They would not write about peace nor would they talk about peace, because their principal reason for being is their struggle for peace, for that peace which is just, true, that will permit them to walk firmly and safely towards the future, free from all enslaving influences that impede the enjoyment of life. Why? What do we understand by peace?...

Jesus did not propagate a legal peace nor a political peace, such as the Pax of Rome, but a different peace altogether. Jesus called and blessed those who seemed anxious for a legal peace, but for whom there was no ray of hope in a middle-class society established in the shadow of the "pax romana." The peace of God that Jesus manifested by means of his communion with sinners, with the poor, and with lepers had non-peaceful effects in that world of order, but also of conflicts. For that reason he was condemned, and was crucified as an enemy of the peace, for he himself was the negation of the gods of their world.

In every study about peace we must constantly ask: peace, for whom? And this question we place in favour of the others, especially those who have no peace or liberty. The same question should convert us into critical elements against those who make peace their exclusive possession to fortify or strengthen their power and increase their goods. . . .

Peace for those who are exploited economically, peace for the despised and the forgotten, peace for those who suffer from oppression, peace for children who die of starvation, for women who have to sell their bodies to eat, peace for the unemployed, peace for the aged, the forgotten, and those who despair. . . .

part 5

the caribbean churches and the way forward

THE CARIBBEAN CHURCHES AND THE WAY FORWARD

The Christian churches in the Caribbean face problems similar to those of individual Christians if they are to take leadership roles in promoting Caribbean unity, development, and spiritual fulfillment. "The Religious Spectrum in the Caribbean" lays out the major difficulties, in the hope that North American Christians especially will reflect upon them in light of their own commitments of faith. "The Story of the Caribbean Conference of Churches" demonstrates the progress already made toward ecumenicity and its continuing thrust, while "A Perspective: Where Do We Go From Here?" concludes the volume with a summary of the situation at present and the hopes of Caribbean Christians for the future.

THE RELIGIOUS SPECTRUM IN THE CARIBBEAN

David Mitchell

The Christian churches in the Caribbean have all come out of missionary work from Europe, either directly or through North American churches. They have often been charged with aiding the imperialist expansions of their nations. Of the Spaniards it was said that upon arriving in the Caribbean they "fell upon their knees and then they fell upon the natives."

The religious divisions of Europe also signalled economic class divisions which the missionary clergy of all the European-derived denominations imposed on the Caribbean. As the example of one young Methodist missionary appointed to the Caribbean in the 1960s illustrates, clergy attitudes often exacerbated other social divisions and tensions. This particular missionary was addicted to "high church" theology, and intensely disliked the laity control found in British Presbyterianism and Congregationalism. So he spent his time in the Caribbean hobnobbing with the "high church" Episcopal clergy at the local cathedral, and refused to have anything to do with the Presbyterian minister and his flock. Since his own congregations, like those of the Episcopal church, were of African descent, while the Presbyterian congregations were of Indian descent, his theological inclinations led him to help maintain the racial and ethnic divisions that riddled that community. He thereby proclaimed his utter indifference to the Gospel imperative that the followers of Christ should reach across the chasms of social division in ministries of reconciliation.

History has left the Caribbean with a very broad and complex religious spectrum. In French-speaking countries (Haiti, Guadeloupe, Martinique, and French Guyana) Roman Catholicism is dominant, as it is in several of the countries which Britain wrested from France and

Spain in the eighteenth and early nineteenth centuries (Trinidad, Grenada, St. Lucia, Dominica, St. Kitts), and in countries that gained independence from Spain (Cuba, the Dominican Republic, and Puerto Rico). But America's 1898 victory in the Spanish-American War opened these Spanish-speaking areas to major American Protestant denominations, with their liberal financial resources, and the Episcopal, United Methodist, United Presbyterian, Disciples of Christ, and Baptist churches were established there.

In English-speaking areas the Anglican (Episcopal) Church predominated, although in Guyana and Jamaica it shared its position with the Presbyterian Church of Scotland. (Upon abolition of slavery in 1838 the British Government made sure that the two state churches would dominate. How many people are aware that Queen Elizabeth II is an Anglican while in England, but becomes a Presbyterian in Scotland?) But these denominations also had competition from missionaries of the British tradesmen's and working men's churches -- Baptist, Congregational, Moravian, and Methodist -- which had been designated "sectarian assemblies" in the eighteenth century.

Little or no communication or cooperation took place between the American branches of Protestantism in the Spanish-speaking Caribbean and the British brands in the English-speaking areas. In the Dutch-speaking regions, Protestantism was of the European continental varieties: Dutch Reformed, Lutheran and Moravian. And the Salvation Army extended its work throughout all language areas.

Further fragmentation arose in the English-speaking regions after the middle nineteenth century, with the ailing sugar industry's importation of large waves of indentured laborers, Hindus and Muslims, from the Calcutta and Madras areas of India. These were isolated on rural plantations and left without formal education or organized religion. The chance visit of John Morton, a young minister of the Presbyterian Church in Canada, who had come in search of a health cure, accidentally opened the door to evangelism among them in 1868. In Trinidad and Guyana, and in the smaller pockets of Indian immigrants in Grenada and St. Lucia, this church pioneered the growth of a Presbyterianism with no structural links to either the Foreign Missions or the Colonial and Continental Committees of the Church of Scotland in Edinburgh. The missionaries in Trinidad elected to join the new United Church of Canada in 1925, while those in Guyana remained with that part of the Presbyterian Church in Canada which did not enter the Union with the Methodists and Congregationalists. Many young East Indian clergymen and other workers were trained in Nova Scotia and Ontario (including Dr. Roy G. Neehall, the present General Secretary of the Caribbean Conference of Churches).

When the nineteenth century white-black conflict in the U.S.A. escalated, producing "black" churches like the A.M.E. and A.M.E. Zion, immigrants from the Caribbean found spiritual homes in them, and developed missionary movements to establish them back in their Caribbean homelands. As the twentieth century continued other American developments of Protestantism taking "holiness" or "pentecostal" forms, like the Disciples of Christ, the Nazarenes, The Church of God (Anderson), the New Testament Church of God, the Wesleyan Holiness (formerly Pilgrim Holiness), the Pentecostal Assemblies, and the Church of the Open Bible, took root in many Caribbean countries, along with deviations from the mainstream of Christianity -- Seventh Day Adventists, Jehovah's Witnesses, Mormons, Christian Science practitioners, Bahais, Rosicrucians, Unity School of Christianity, and others. A veritable welter of beliefs had descended on the Caribbean.

Meanwhile the survival of African religious practices was reinforced by slaves landed in the Caribbean after their release by the British navy from slaveships of nations still continuing the trade in the nineteenth century. These practices were combined with the rituals of the Roman Catholic Church and with Protestant hymns to express the cultic practices of indigenous religious groups -- voodoo in Haiti, Pocomania in Jamaica, Shango in Trinidad and Grenada, the rites of the "Spiritual Baptists" of Trinidad and St. Vincent, and area-wide religious rites like funeral wakes, healing "bathing" and anointing ceremonies.

And Hindu and Muslim immigrants had developed a chain of temples and mosques in Surinam, Guyana, Trinidad, Jamaica, and Barbados. The last two or three generations of Indian immigrants had been compelled to attend Christian denominational schools and to submit to the teaching of Christian scripture, so a good deal of admixture took place. Hindus have adapted several elements of the Christian faith and church structures, and now run Sunday schools to teach Hindu beliefs. In a temple compound in one Trinidad village there is even a small Hindu shrine dedicated to "Father, Son, and Holy Spirit." Some years ago the weekly religious T.V. program on Trinidad and Tobago Television was called Church Unity, though Hindu and Muslim groups shared in the allocation of sessions. Attempts to establish an ecumenical house of prayer shared by Christians, Muslims and Hindus led to the founding of the Inter-Religious Organization encompassing the three faiths, with which the Trinidad and Tobago government or other organizations can deal.

But on the whole the many Caribbean churches remain very divided. World-wide trends toward ecumenism have had good local effects, but three main problems confront us.

The first is the continuing complete isolation of churches with missionary origins in the United States from those of European derivations. Whether the churches are Roman Catholic, Anglican (or Episcopal), Methodist, Reformed or Moravian, great gaps of silence exist between their different geographical brands. It seems very strange that Methodists with British origins should feel closer to Roman Catholics in their midst than to fellow-Methodists from the United States.

Next, language barriers pose difficult problems in a region where English, French, Spanish and Dutch are official languages, but are like foreign tongues to the masses of rural and urban workers who speak mixed vernaculars of African and European forms and vocabulary. These may be Creole (African and French), as in Haiti, the French Antilles, Dominica, St. Lucia, and Trinidad; or Papiamento (African and Portuguese), as in Curacao and Aruba, or Sranan (African and English), as in Surinam, or Jamaican. And except in Haiti, where there is a literacy program, vernacular dialects are not read. There is no visual teaching of them in the schools. In addition, the elite middle classes often object to the use of the vernacular in religious sermons, hymns and liturgies.

And third, we have hardly begun to ask what theology the Caribbean churches should propound. When we apply the Gospel to our Caribbean situation, what loyalties and what actions does God reveal to us? Such thinkers as William Watty, President of the United Theological College of the West Indies in Jamaica, (see"Struggling to Be," in this volume) and Jacinto Ordonez of Cuba, among others, have begun to raise this question forcefully in recent years, and to warn us that we must recognize and confront it if we would let God speak to us at this time in our history. But a great deal more effort remains before us if we are to see the full emergence of a truly Caribbean theology.

While we are struggling with these problems we hope to help North Americans see them too, and with them some of the dilemmas which God is now throwing in the paths of North American Christians. Isn't He asking them to apply their own experiences of His presence, to arouse their own faith, to confront our mutual problems, and to take action?

THE STORY OF THE CARIBBEAN CONFERENCE OF CHURCHES

Kortright Davis

Ecumenical cooperation among non-Anglican Protestant churches in the Caribbean began in the early decades of the twentieth century with the formation of national Evangelical Councils of Churches and Sunday School Associations, but without Caribbean-wide organization.

During World War II, however, comprehensive surveys of the region were undertaken,[1] and in Puerto Rico in 1957 some denominations responded to an invitation from the former International Missionary Council and the World Council of Christian Education. They consulted on their needs and objectives, and defined five areas of need: Christian Education, Theological Education, Home and Family Life, Evangelism, especially among Hindus and Muslims, and special South Caribbean problems.[2]

In 1959 some of the denominations held a Curriculum Conference in Jamaica and formed the Caribbean Committee for Joint Christian Action (CCJCA), a representative working group under David Mitchell, a Grenada-born Methodist minister. CCJCA developed a number of regional programs, and was particularly instrumental in producing an innovative series of publications for Sunday schools, in a style based on Caribbean life.[3] Its Family Life Education Program developed a number of national committees throughout the region, and a West Indian clergy-

---

(1) See E.J. Bingle, *From Cuba to Surinam*, (N.Y. and London: International Missionary Council, 1955). Private circulation.

(2) See *The Listening Isles Report of the 1957 Ecumenical Consultation in Puerto Rico*, (N.Y. and London: International Missionary Council and World Council of Christian Education, 1958).

(3) See reference to Caribbean "Christian Living" Curriculum Series in *With Eyes Wide Open*, ed. David Mitchell, (Barbados: CADEC, 1973), pp. 192 ff., 198.

man and his wife were provided with a bursary in the United States for specialized training in family counselling. They returned in 1969 and set up a center in Jamaica.

The need for more concrete social action was continually felt by Caribbean church leaders, who by this time were more or less native to the area.[4] Many agreed that the church had to become more relevant to the needs and aspirations of the masses of Caribbean people, whose values and lifestyles had so far been related to cultures and societies which were foreign to them. And the churches were increasingly being accused of sustaining these alienating influences. Further, it was being recognized that the churches had resources which could be better used in helping the people of the Caribbean to help themselves.

Out of these concerns came a new agency, Christian Action for Development in the Caribbean (CADEC), founded in 1968 with the help of the Church World Service agency of the National Council of Churches in the U.S.A. CADEC's growth was pioneered by Rev. Robert Cuthbert, a Jamaican pastor in the Moravian church.[5] Its objectives were to respond to the deepest needs of the Caribbean people, primarily to develop a spirit of self-dependence and renunciation of other people's initiatives. The churches were to spell out in simple terms the various factors hindering human growth in the Caribbean and to attack them as best they could with the resources at their disposal, while trying to secure more material resources to assist groups of marginal people in their own self-development. These programs would differ from traditional welfare-type operations whereby people positioned themselves to continual receiving of aid from others. The churches were to commit themselves to dispelling the myth that Caribbean people were lazy and unable to help themselves.

Beyond this, it was obvious that most decisions vital to Caribbean communities were made by very small elites, and that the majority of people lacked participation and interest in national affairs. The Caribbean's political legacy has tended to make the masses of its people into mere audiences, watching the dramas of politicians and other decision-makers without response. CADEC therefore determined to raise the critical consciousness of the people in general and to provide critical analyses of national issues in particular. Various ecumenical action

---

(4) D. Mitchell, ed., *With Eyes Wide Open*, p. 187.

(5) D. Mitchell. *op cit.*, pp. 194, 195.

groups were also brought together under the aegis of CADEC, and integration and coordination commenced.

Ecumenical history was made in November, 1973, when some 19 churches joined in forming the Caribbean Conference of Churches. The Inaugural Assembly took place in Kingston, Jamaica, and was particularly significant because for the first time the Roman Catholic Church became a founding member of a regional ecumenical body. The occasion was also significant for the wide variety of cultural, linguistic, and denominational backgrounds which converged in a formal affirmation of their common concerns and destiny:

> "We as Christian people of the Caribbean, separated from each other by barriers of history, language, culture, class and distance, desire, because of our common calling to Christ, to join together in a regional fellowship of Churches for inspiration, consultation, and co-operative action.
>
> "We are deeply concerned to promote the human liberation of our people, and are committed to the achievement of social justice and the dignity of man in our society. We desire to build up together our life in Christ and to share our experience with the universal brotherhood of mankind."

The Caribbean Conference of Churches embraced the work of CCJCA and CADEC. It resolved itself into two commissions, Renewal and Development, to carry out the broad mandate from its member churches.

The Renewal Commission deals with programs and issues which affect the life and work of the Christian Church in a changing age. It functions through its agency, Action for Renewal of the Church (ARC), under the direction of Fr. Kelvin Felix, a Roman Catholic priest from Dominica. It is primarily responsible for programs in Evangelism, Theological Renewal, Caribbean Identity, Women's Work, Youth Affairs, Christian Education, Family Life Education, and Caribbean Church Music.

The Development Commission retains CADEC as its agency, with Robert Cuthbert continuing as Director. It deals with programs and issues which catalyze the full human development of Caribbean cultures, and is responsible for Project Development, Caribbean Community Appeal, Education for Development, Scholarships, and Communications. CADEC also sponsors a Development Fund, supported by contributions from churches and agencies both within and outside the Caribbean, through which project requests from the entire region are funded.

Two other Caribbean Conference of Churches agencies have been created to help meet the communication needs of the Caribbean people. *Caribbean Contact*, a monthly regional journal, examines issues and episodes that concern the Caribbean in detail. Cedar Press is a publishing house committed to developing Caribbean literature and the skills of Caribbean writers. Since both are engaged in commercial-type operations, they are private nonprofit companies.

The CCC services its programs through six centers spread around the Caribbean and a staff of about 70. Its programs are generally geared to respond to needs and initiatives of the Caribbean people themselves, and to support the ongoing work of Christian churches. It functions principally as a service organization run by and for its member churches, and provides novel ways for assisting them to interpret their roles and calls to mission in the world. Spearheading the whole movement is Trinidadian Dr. Roy G. Neehall, General Secretary of the CCC, supported by the three Presidents; Archbishop Carter of the R.C. Church, President C. Cadogan of the Methodist Church, and Mrs. Dorinda Sampath of the Presbyterian Church.[6]

Support for the work of the CCC has been slow in coming from the Caribbean itself, as most churches appear to be more preoccupied with their own programs. But this is not surprising in view of the histories of the denominations. Neither is it surprising that the general drain of profits from the Caribbean economy to the foreign shareholders (many of whom are Christians) of metropolitan corporations, which prevents accumulation of capital in the Caribbean, also prevents the adequate endowment of the Caribbean's churches and charitable institutions, which now have to create infrastructures of their own to sustain their increasing autonomy. In this connection CCC's public interpretations of its role and actions are generating more support for the Caribbean Community Appeal.

In addition, liberal aid is being offered by ecumenical and other funding agencies and foundations. But since it comes largely from metropolitan sources, this appears as a recycling, through the programs of CCC, of some of the profit which multi-national exploitation has siphoned from the Caribbean economy.

---

(6) Caribbean Conference of Churches, "Report of the Inaugural Assembly," (Mimeo), Barbados, 1973, p. 40.

But in spite of the practical dilemmas which face the ecumenical movement in the Caribbean, the story of the Caribbean Conference of Churches shows a dawning recognition on the part of Christians that the future of the Caribbean Church can only be ONE.

A PERSPECTIVE: WHERE DO WE GO FROM HERE?

David Mitchell

What of the Caribbean churches and the way forward?

North American and British denominations that have given us traditional kinds of missionary support have done much to help us meet several challenges, particularly in Haiti, where the need for human development is greatest and the government is weakest, financially and in technical skills.

But more important, since 1950 these denominations have been transferring responsibility to national church leaders in the Caribbean. Legal autonomy has been granted to Caribbean churches. Grants for administration have been placed on a reducing basis, and new grants have been made for new forms of ministry, new types of programs, designed to make the ministries of Christian churches more relevant to the Caribbean's needs for human development. These grants are increasingly being made not on bilateral bases between metropolitan denominations and their Caribbean offspring, but on ecumenical bases between metropolitan denominations and National Councils of Churches or the Caribbean Conference of Churches.

These developments respond well to the need of Caribbean Christians to build the infrastructures necessary to run their own denominations, rather than having them run by missionary departments in New York, Toronto, Indianapolis, or elsewhere. But in view of the decisions of the British, Canadian, Dutch, French and U.S. governments and business interests to use our resources, our raw materials, virtually to subsidize their economies, Caribbean church leaders are becoming less inclined to view grants from metropolitan churches as handouts. As Kortright Davis emphasized in "The Story of the Caribbean Conference of Churches," we are increasingly seeing such grants as recycling into our area a small part of the capital that has been taken out of it by international trading and manufacturing organizations, who have distributed Caribbean-derived profits to their shareholders -- among whom happen to be individual church members and national denominational finance departments.

The transfer of responsibility to Caribbean church leaders has sometimes been accompanied by an emotional problem. As local leaders emerge, expatriate clergy who may have been our intimate personal friends are withdrawn. They may have been friends, true -- but they have done things their way, and not as we have deemed necessary. It is very hard to tell a friend, especially one who represents or holds metropolitan money bags, "Get off my back and give me a chance to do things my way." He has come to help, and finds it hard to see our situation from our point of view.[1] This is likely also to be true of his replacement, the CUSO (Canadian), VSO (British) or Peace Corps (USA) volunteer,[2] who is equally unequipped to understand that one of our deepest problems is the feeling of so many people that it is wrong to challenge white expatriates or say *no* to them. . . a problem hardly surprising among peoples who have grown up under centuries of believing European or American ways of doing things, of worship, of singing, of dress, culture, etc., are the *only* ways.

And withdrawal of expatriate missionary staffs has also involved withdrawal of funds to support workers who have been filling gaps, doing jobs, albeit from the wrong standpoints or understandings. With their withdrawal the gaps remain unfilled.

Since Vatican II in the early 1960s, and with the general search among Christians for inter-communion and forms of unity among the world denominations, it has been easier for us to work with our Christian brothers at national council and Caribbean-wide levels. And our attention has repeatedly turned to programs, projects and actions aimed at relieving poverty and giving skills and hope to the helpless.

---

(1) The Caribbean Conference of Churches, *Christians in Dialogue and Joint Action: Report of a Consultation on the Ecumenical Sharing of Personnel,* Barbados, 1975, pp. 7, 9, 11, 26, 28, 35, 37.

(2) In the latter half of the twentieth century initiatives came from Canada, Britain, and the U.S.A. by which university undergraduates or graduates give help to government or private groups in various fields--education, community development, and the like. These volunteers were required to live among the people of the area at minimum salaries, without the usual affluent or ostentatious life-styles usually displayed by Europeans or North Americans.

But increasingly we are realizing that even these priorities do not reach to the roots of the Caribbean's problems. Why help local fishermen to fish better, preserve and distribute their catches better, when multi-national corporations cut them out of servicing local supermarkets, multi-national supermarket chains, and hotels? Against such pressures genuine local industries have very little chance of developing to reduce local poverty and starvation. Under these conditions, is it any wonder that so many of us are turning away from the "great American Dream" of raising our standards of living and instead are struggling to free ourselves from the metropolitan strangle-knot?

It is no good saying we ought to have known better, that we shouldn't have let ourselves be manipulated and fooled, that countries get the freedom and the economies they deserve. The damage has been done, and we are caught in its continuing squeeze. We are now compelled to act to free ourselves.

Neither is it any good warning us of the bogey of Communism, or declaiming to us the advantages of "free enterprise." The present multi-national system is not free enterprise, the free flow of market forces determining prices. It is nothing like the economists' reminiscences of nineteenth century capitalism. We know we are expendable pawns in the fierce economic contests of the last quarter of the twentieth century. We can see ourselves getting poorer and the northern hemisphere civilizations getting richer, and we know their profit margins could not be so high if they had not forced ours so low.

We are beginning to realize that modern capitalism has not given us what we need. Who has the right to blame some of us if we try other systems, even socialist? What is there to lose for those who do try other systems?

So we take our first faltering steps of awareness in the jungle-conflict which is modern civilization. It gives us deep satisfaction to try to be ourselves, to "do our own thing" -- in worship, in culture, in economic development, in education, in human development, in life.

Because of our overriding needs for the liberation of our culture, our environment, our ecology -- all the structures of our society -- for our own use, certain issues of current importance in North America and Europe appear as subsidiary ones in our list of priorites. Our women need to be liberated in many ways, yet we have not singled out women's liberation for discussion in this volume. We face a generation gap between youth and adults that differs from previous inter-generational conflicts. The effects of modern technology -- traffic roar, neon signs, "time-bound" systems that tie us to inexorably crushing routines, factory and equipment noise levels -- have given the nervous system and physical senses of our children different mental and emotional patterns and responses from those of adults who grew up in the more rural and pastoral age that receded rapidly after the 1920s. Yet this volume's spokesman for youth has not dwelt upon a generation gap as metropolitan North Atlantic society understands it, but rather on the total system which makes Caribbean youth marginal and dispensable. We could have looked more closely at the rights of the cultures that can be regarded as indigenous -- the Amerindian cultures of the Arawaks, Caribs, and Indian tribes of Central and South America. We could also have drawn attention to the exploitation of minorities. We could have focussed on the various ways racism of all sorts is practiced here.

But in the end these problems remain aspects, symptoms really, of the malaise of our Caribbean world, and we have addressed ourselves to what we consider the most basic causes and most general manifestations of that malaise. And we now ask our readers, Do you begin to understand us better? Do you desire to help us out of our predicament? Can our predicament and our awareness of it help you with yours? What will be the costs, to us and to you, of acting on our awareness? Where do our Christian responsibilities and discipleship lie? Where do yours lie?

And if North American readers are moved to ask, "What can our churches do to help?" Perhaps the only answer we can give is -- Enter into dialogue with us, and into the relationships our situations require. Let us expose our preconceptions, assumptions, biases and prejudices to the searching presence of our common Lord and his truth. Only He frees and unites. Let us act, as individuals, as congregations, as denominations, as Christian communities, on the light and insights He gives. Let us "keep abreast of truth," for the Holy Spirit will never end the growth of our insights. May growth of all sorts be with us and with you, until we pass on and until the end of time.

About the Contributors

Oscar Allen left teaching in his home country of St. Vincent, W.I. to study for the Methodist ministry in Jamaica. He interrupted his studies to serve in a rural pastorate in Haiti. His insights, gained from that experience, led to a demand for more relevant forms of training as a pastor, especially in agriculture. The challenge was not able to produce the change in training, and he now serves privately as a rural organizer and animator of youth groups in his native St. Vincent.

Sergio Arce-Martinez is President of the Matanzas United Theological Seminary.

Rev. Claude Cadogan is a Belizean-born Methodist minister. He has worked extensively in Jamaica and Belize, holding top positions in the Synods there. He is now coming to the end of his five-year term as President of the Conference of the Methodist Church in the Caribbean and the Americas.

Kortright Davis is from Antigua, West Indies. He trained for the Anglican priesthood in Barbados, where he married and now lives. After service on the staff of Codrington Theological College, Barbados, he joined the Caribbean Conference of Churches as sub-regional coordinator of CCC programs in the Leeward Islands region from a base in Antigua. He subsequently transferred back to Barbados as head of the Project Development Department of the Conference, still finding time to serve the pulpits of his denomination. He now is Secretary of the Committee responsible for organizing the 1977 Assembly of the Caribbean Conference of Church held in Guyana in November 1977.

P.I. Gomes was born and educated in Guyana. He became a Jesuit priest and for several years he was attached to GISRA (The Guyana Institute of Social and Religious Action). Requesting permission to become a layman again, he now works in the Faculty of Agriculture, University of the West Indies, St. Augustine, Trinidad.

Anthony Gonzales is a Roman Catholic layman on the staff of the Institute of International Relations, University of the West Indies, St. Augustine, Trinidad. He hails from the Southern Caribbean area. His academic interests center around the external trade relations of Caribbean states.

Irene Hawkins was born in West Germany, where she studied economics and business and worked for the Deutsche Bank head office. She married and settled in her husband's country, Britain. There, she served for three years on the editorial staff of *The Economist*. While living in Barbados in 1970-71 she visited many of the English-speaking Caribbean countries and wrote on a wide range of social and economic subjects. Her writings and research have covered Caribbean affairs in all four language areas (English, Spanish, French and Dutch), European affairs, tourism and the aluminum industry. She has been a consultant at the B.B.C. on a series of European Common Market programs.

Carol Keller was a high school teacher in his native country, Trinidad. After studying at the Trinidad campus of the University of the West Indies, he did post-

About the Contributors

graduate work in the Institute of International Relations. He now lectures in that field of study.

Pere Oscar La Croix moved from Roman Catholic parish work to teaching and then to youth work in his native Guadeloupe. He has studied in Lyons and Paris. Presently, he is responsible for the catechetical program in the diocese, serves as Vicar-General to his Bishop and is responsible for ecumenical relations.

Neville Linton, Guyanese, has studied and lectured in North America. For several years he has been lecturing at the Institute of International Relations, the University of the West Indies, St. Augustine, Trinidad.

Ivan Meléndez-Acosta, a native of Puerto Rico, is a university professor. He has served in the Department of Education of the Commonwealth of Puerto Rico, in the Caribbean Center for Advanced Religious Studies, the Sacred Heart University College and the College of Natural Sciences in the University of Puerto Rico. He was selected as one of the 'outstanding young men of America' for 1976. He is a Roman Catholic.

Pere Serge Plaucoste is a young Guadeloupean Roman Catholic priest with university training. He has worked in industry, in hospitals and in building constructions. He has been assigned to chaplaincy work in trade unions, and has been especially active among youth sections of trade unions. He has visited Haiti, Puerto Rico and Santo Domingo.

Alfred C. Reid is a Jamaican-born Anglican priest who studied for the priesthood in his home country. He has been serving in sensitive urban and lower-class suburban parishes in Kingston.

Jimmy Tucker, Jamaican-born, has studied theology and law. In 1973 he joined the staff of the Caribbean Conference of Churches as sub-regional coordinator of the northwest Caribbean region programmes and was stationed in Jamaica. His area covered Belize, Bahamas and Jamaica, with responsibility for contacts with Cuba, Haiti and the Dominican Republic. He has now been appointed to the Human Rights desk of CCC.

William W. Watty, was born in Dominica, West Indies. He studied for the Methodist ministry in Jamaica and served in the British Virgin Islands and in Trinidad. His University studies were at London and Birmingham Universities, where he served in the British Student Christian Movement. He later became a tutor in the British ecumenical missionary training complex at Selly Oak, Birmingham. After this he became Methodist warden and ministerial tutor at the United Theological College of the West Indies in Jamaica. He is now Principal of that College.